# YOU CAN WIN!

## Roger Campbell

*Presented By*
*Scripture Press Ministries*
*Glen Ellyn, Illinois, U.*

While this book is designed for the reader's personal use and profit, it is also intended for group study. A leader's guide is available from your local bookstore or from the publisher.

**VICTOR**

**BOOKS** a division of SP Publications, Inc.
WHEATON, ILLINOIS 60187

*Offices also in*
Whitby, Ontario, Canada
Amersham-on-the-Hill, Bucks, England

Bible quotations are from the *King James Version*.

Recommended Dewey Decimal Classification: 248.4
Suggested Subject Headings: CHRISTIAN LIFE; SPIRITUAL LIFE

Library of Congress Catalog Card Number: 84-52047
ISBN: 0-88207-317-0

# CONTENTS

To Graham and Shannon

# PREFACE

These are days of pressure and peril. The fast pace of the age and the lifestyles most have chosen are taking their toll on us.

Lurking in the shadows is the everpresent threat of nuclear war. We sleep and wake and go about our daily tasks zeroed into the missile sights of military powers bent on our destruction.

Mind-boggling discoveries and inventions flood in upon us. Some of these acclaimed breakthroughs relieve suffering and extend life while others pose hazards unknown to all who have come before us.

Modern communications have plugged us into the trouble spots of the whole world. Television allows us to witness violence around the world almost as soon as it happens.

In *You Can Win* I call for believers to use the resources our Lord has provided for coping in any age. We do not have to be victims of the times. Nothing takes God by surprise; He has given us all we need for daily victory whatever our circumstances may be.

Most of us live far below our potential.

It is my prayer that some of the thoughts I share here will lead discouraged readers on to higher ground.

# ONE
# YES, YOU CAN!

An opportunity has just come your way. All you have to do is accept and the position is yours. One phone call and a whole new world of work or service will open to you. The ball is in your court.

You're thrilled, but apprehensive.

Not that you wouldn't enjoy the challenge. You've been praying for some kind of breakthrough that would allow you to make full use of your gifts and abilities. But right now you're paralyzed by negatives; unwanted questions are surfacing.

Can you handle the responsibility?

Will others accept your leadership or approve of your work?

Will you come through or be a disappointment?

Might you cave in under pressure?

Do you really have what it takes to do the job?

## JOSHUA'S CHALLENGE

Long ago, Joshua, of wall-falling fame, must have felt much as you do. Born a slave, he had been appointed leader of his people. They had arrived at the border of Canaan, the land they had longed to enter for more than a generation. The greater part of that time had been given to wandering about in the desert as a result of their unbelief and unwillingness to occupy the land forty years earlier. Now it was time for them to move forward and claim what God had promised them so many years before.

Moses, their great deliverer and leader, was dead. Before his death, he had revealed that Joshua, his minister, was to succeed him and lead the Children of Israel into the Promised Land (Deut. 31:1-8).

But conquering Canaan would not be an easy task. The Canaanites were numerous and powerful. The very sight of them had frightened most of the spies sent forth into the land by Moses a generation earlier, and as a result they brought back a negative report, advising the people not to advance as had been planned. Only Caleb and Joshua had urged the Israelites to move ahead in faith expecting victory, but they were overruled by the doubters who were in the majority (Num. 13:27-33).

In addition to the obstacles before him, Joshua must have considered the military potential of the company he was to lead. Their record was poor. Over and over again they had acted faithlessly and had been chronic complainers against Moses.

Could he, as their new leader, expect better treatment? Probably not.

The first nine verses of the Book of Joshua record the Lord's commission to this prospective new leader concerning his position and responsibilities. This divine commission demands courage, faith, and action and promises success. It contains principles that will be helpful to anyone needing encouragement to face a new challenge.

### GETTING ON THE MOVE

God's first instruction to Joshua called for him to be decisive and get on the move: "Moses My servant is dead; now therefore arise, go over this Jordan, thou, and all this people, unto the land which I do give to them, even to the Children of Israel" (Josh. 1:2).

The loss of Moses had been traumatic both for Joshua and his people. Meek but mighty through God's power, Moses had interceded for these erring people time and again, bringing water from a rock when they were thirsty and praying down manna when they ran out of food. He had been with God on Mount Sinai and had received the Law that was to be their standard of righteousness. Though they had rebelled against him many times, they were in awe of him and at his death went into mourning for thirty days.

Now Joshua had been called to replace him.

Some order.

Nevertheless, it was God's order. Servants of God may move or die but His work must go on.

Joshua may have struggled with this aspect of his call. How could he replace Moses?

He was not like Moses.

No matter.

God would use him in a different way.

If Moses had been the only person capable of leading Israel into Canaan, he would doubtless have been spared for that purpose. But he was not spared. An outburst of temper causing disobedience had cost him the privilege of leading his people into the Promised Land. And Joshua was now God's man for the occasion. He was not to fill the shoes of Moses. His was a new call. He would not be expected to do things just as Moses had done them, but he must expect God to use him in a unique way to accomplish the task at hand.

"Go over this Jordan," was the command.

Inadequate as Joshua felt, he must get moving. In spite of the dangers ahead, he must move. Unless he moves forward, he will never receive the blessings that await him. If he sits and broods over the possibility of failure, he will never conquer Canaan—never enter the Promised Land.

## HEADING TOWARD GOALS

Christian Powell had longed to become an attorney. He had set this ambitious goal early in life but was afflicted by two dreaded diseases: tuberculosis and polio. Both diseases hospitalized him for long periods of time, and the latter paralyzed most of the major muscles in the lower part of his body. When he was discharged from the hospital after his bout with polio at the age of nineteen, there seemed little hope that he could catch up academically or even go to college, let alone tackle the rigorous and expensive course leading to a law degree.

But Christian Powell wouldn't concede defeat. He had a dream and was unwilling to settle for a nightmare. Spending many hours each day building up his upper body and studying, he kept pressing toward his goal. One year later, he enrolled in a special college prep course that allowed him to get his high school diploma, and ten years after that walked across a graduation platform to receive his law degree. By that time he was married, the father of four sons, and already successful in the field of accounting.

Within a few years after receiving his law degree, Powell was the managing partner in a growing law firm and was active politically and as a land developer. Today, in addition to being involved in several business ventures, he is teaching in a Bible institute.

Why has he been successful?

One of the most important reasons has been his practice of starting toward the high goals he has set for himself.

Success begins in beginning.

## GREAT EXPECTATIONS

Joshua had to start moving and expect to conquer; he had to think big. Note this thrilling promise that would be activated as soon as he started advancing: "Every place that the sole of your foot shall tread upon, that have I given unto you, as I said unto Moses" (Josh. 1:3). This promise does not apply to sitters—only those on the move. A speaker at a church building dedication service challenged the congregation with the above text. The title of his sermon was, "How Big Are Your Feet?"

Most of us do not accomplish much because we do not expect to accomplish very much. A.B. Simpson indicted the majority of us when he said, "Our God has boundless resources. The only limit is in us. Our asking, our thinking, our praying are too small. Our expectations are too limited."[1] J. Hudson Taylor observed, "Many Christians estimate difficulties in the light of their own resources, and thus attempt little and often fail in the little they attempt."[2]

Marching into the Promised Land would mean danger. Canaan would not be conquered quickly. There would be long marches and protracted campaigns. Some days would not be long enough for the battles. . . . One would have to be lengthened. There would be some defeats along the way to ultimate victory. But life is like that, especially the Christian life. And any challenge worth taking involves giving every ounce of strength to win. In her book *Ms. Means Myself*, Gladys Hunt writes:

> Adventure or creativity—whichever word you like best—always involves risks. It involves a decision; it is purposive; it is an expression of yourself. Usually, it involves others. It stretches you, so that you end up being more than you ever thought you could be. It adds the special flavor to life that makes you feel that you have a secret with God.[3]

## GOD GOES WITH US

By this time, Joshua was probably trembling; he was feeling small. Moses might have been up to this task but not Joshua. He was comparing himself to his human ideal and felt he didn't measure up. So God encouraged him; He let him know that he would not be expected to fight these battles in his own strength. "There shall not any man be able to stand before thee all the days of thy life: as I was with Moses, so I will be with thee; I will not fail thee, nor forsake thee" (Josh.1:5). God is the great equalizer. His presence makes the difference.

A shepherd boy named David can face the huge hero of the Philistines because God is with him. Daniel is safe among the lions because God is with him. Three young Hebrew captives in Babylon survive the fiery furnace of the king because God goes through the fire with them. A handful of uneducated disciples reach thousands for Christ in the hostile city of Jerusalem and ultimately become known as world-upsetters because God is with them.

God seems to delight in taking those who are ill equipped

by the world's standards and making them eminently successful. Peter and John were called unlearned and ignorant, but even their enemies knew they had been with Jesus and that His power was operative in their lives (Acts 4:13).

A.W. Neale had to leave school in the seventh grade to help support his family. He worked in a lumber yard twelve hours a day, six days a week. An alert insurance salesman noted his cheerfulness even on tough assignments and offered him a position in his office. In his twenties, Neale received Christ as his Saviour and applied himself both to developing in the Christian life and to his work. Before long, he was able to buy the insurance agency and was so successful that even the Great Depression couldn't wipe him out. Missionaries found a ready listener in A.W. Neale as well as a ready check-writer. God had found a diligent man whom He could trust, and He blessed him in spite of his lack of formal education.

## STRENGTH FOR WEAKNESS

Contemplating the responsibilities of his new position, Joshua evidently felt weak and afraid. Three times during his commissioning he was told to be strong and courageous:

> Be strong and of a good courage, for unto this people shalt thou divide for an inheritance the land, which I sware unto their fathers to give them. Only be thou strong and very courageous, that thou mayest observe to do according to all the Law, which Moses My servant commanded thee. Turn not from it to the right hand or to the left, that thou mayest prosper whithersoever thou goest. . . . Have not I commanded thee? Be strong and of a good courage; be not afraid, neither be thou dismayed: for the Lord thy God is with thee whithersoever thou goest (Josh. 1:6-7, 9).

Most of us can identify with weakness and fear. Few escape trembling times. But we should remember that God has tipped the scales in favor of many a weak one and made him or her a success.

George Frederick Handel lost his health; his right side was

paralyzed; his money was gone, and his creditors threatened to imprison him. Handel was so disheartened by his situation that he almost despaired. But his faith prevailed. In his affliction, he composed his greatest work, "The Hallelujah Chorus," which is part of his great "Messiah."

The list is long of those who have overcome handicaps and gone on to achievement and success through trust in the Lord. Annie Johnson Flint, afflicted with pain and suffering, wrote the much used "He Giveth More Grace" and many other wonderful poems. Fanny Crosby was blind but composed 8,000 published hymns. Helen Keller, shortly before her sixtieth birthday, expressed pity for the real unseeing, for those who have eyes still often do not see. She said, "If the blind put their hand in God's, they find their way more surely than those who see but have not faith or purpose."[4]

Joshua needed to understand that his strength would come from his Lord who is never weary or faint. "Be strong" is an impossible command to obey unless our God imparts His strength to us. And He does.

> He giveth power to the faint, and to them that have no might He increaseth strength. Even the youths shall faint and be weary, and the young men shall utterly fall; but they that wait upon the Lord shall renew their strength; they shall mount up with wings as eagles; they shall run, and not be weary; and they shall walk and not faint (Isa. 40:29-31).

## GOD IS ABLE

Life teaches us our limits. There are problems too complicated for us to solve, burdens too heavy for us to bear, work too difficult for us to do. But God is able to do all things. And He can pour His strength into us. That is why Paul could write, "I can do all things through Christ who strengtheneth me" (Phil. 4:13).

Weakness and fear are troublesome twins.

Fear is a monster that stalks us all. It brings depression, stifles ability, and robs life of its adventure. No wonder God kept repeating His call for Joshua to be courageous.

But, humanly speaking, Joshua had reason to fear.

He was being called to a task that seemed far beyond his ability. He was about to embark on the fulfilling of a former dream that had once appeared to be within his grasp and then had escaped. He was not young anymore. And thousands of others would be depending on him.

The Jordan River must be crossed and that was only the beginning. After crossing the Jordan, the Children of Israel would encounter Jericho, the great walled city that had withstood attacks by forces far more powerful than any Israel could muster. Beyond Jericho were other cities and areas defended by strong and warlike people whose very appearance had caused ten of the original spies sent by Moses to cringe with fear and feel as small as grasshoppers (Num. 13:33).

How could he acquire the courage needed for this assignment?

## DRAWING ON PAST VICTORIES

One source might have been remembering a spiritual mountain peak in his past; a time when he was able to trust God completely while others doubted.

Forty years earlier, when he had been one of the spies chosen by Moses to scout the Promised Land, his faith had soared at seeing the bounty there. The land was all that God had said it would be. Out of the twelve sent, however, only he and Caleb had urged Israel to advance. When the doubters were calling upon the people to retreat, he had joined Caleb in calling for faith.

He had dared to trust while the majority trembled.

Now he could look back to that high day and summon great faith again. You can almost see the fire in his eyes as he spans forty years and feels the decades drop away. For a moment he is a young man, challenging his people to march forward and claim the land (Num. 14:8-9).

Others have had places to which they returned in person or memory to rehearse God's blessings and refresh their faith. Jacob returned to Bethel, a place where he had met God in a special way and made commitments to Him. John Wesley preached a powerful sermon from his father's gravestone while an angry crowd bloodied his face with flying objects.

Often, in thought, I kneel near the creek that flows through the pasture of the farm where I lived as a boy and there I pour out my heart to God. Sometimes when I hear a congregation sing, "Where He Leads Me," I feel again the burning of hot tears that welled up in my eyes as I walked down a church aisle to publicly acknowledge my surrender to Christ. Remembering these special times builds my faith and sends me on to serve the Lord with renewed vigor.

## GOD'S FAITHFULNESS

Joshua may also have nourished courage by turning his thoughts from the dangers ahead to God's faithfulness in the past. He had survived forty years of wandering in the wilderness while nearly all the others of his generation had died. God had been true to His promise. He could expect the same consistency of divine care in the future.

Near the end of his life, J. Hudson Taylor wrote to a friend saying that he was so feeble that he could not work, read his Bible, or even pray. He said he could only lie still in God's arms like a little child and trust. But in his childlike faith Taylor was free from fear in spite of his weakness.

## THE POWER OF GOD'S WORD

Another source of courage for Joshua was be the Word of God. Strategically located between two calls for courage is this vital verse: "This book of the Law shall not depart out of thy mouth; but thou shalt meditate therein day and night, that thou mayest observe to do according to all that is written therein, for then thou shalt make thy way prosperous, and then thou shalt have good success" (Josh. 1:8).

Faith grows through exposure to the Bible. This was true in Joshua's day and it is true now: "So then faith cometh by hearing, and hearing by the Word of God" (Rom. 10:17).

God's promises encourage faith. As you take time to study the Bible, you will find guarantees of strength, peace, courage, salvation, power, victory, and answered prayer. You will read of exploits of others who have conquered through faith. As you identify with these promises and personal triumphs, your faith will increase. Depression will depart. Expectation will emerge. Courage for tough tasks will grow.

To whatever degree Joshua was able to rest on God's promises and in His love, he overcame the fears he harbored about leading his people into Canaan. And that will always be true for each of us as we seek to conquer our anxieties. "There is no fear in love; but perfect love casteth out fear, because fear hath torment. He that feareth is not made perfect in love" (1 John 4:18).

## DON'T MISS YOUR GREATEST HOUR

Had Joshua refused his commission because of fear or feelings of inadequacy, he would have made a terrible mistake. Turning down this opportunity would have robbed him of the greatest adventure of his life. Out of fear, he might have missed out on the fulfilling of his life's dream. Frightening as it may sound, he could have bypassed the purpose for which he was born.

Take care that you don't bypass yours.

Joshua would have missed crossing the Jordan at floodtide, seeing this mighty river open before him. Be sure you don't miss the greatest spiritual breakthrough of your life.

Joshua would have missed seeing the walls of Jericho fall down. Don't miss the tumbling of barriers that keep you and your family from God's best.

Joshua would have missed leading his people to multiplied triumphs and watching them possess what God had promised them. Make sure you don't miss bringing other people to Christ and watching them grow to spiritual maturity.

Joshua would never have discovered that in the time of need God could actually supply him with the courage and strength needed for conflict with his foes. You don't want to miss the thrill of sensing you are in the perfect will of God and that He is doing through you what you never would have been able to do alone.

Joshua did not miss out.

He accepted the challenge and won.

So can you.

Really. You can.

# TWO

# *ENLARGE YOUR TERRITORY*

Each morning I stand before a large map on my study wall and repeat a prayer from the Old Testament. This prayer is found in a chapter that one might be tempted to skip over when reading through the Bible because it is largely a list of the names of people and their descendants. But there is a gem among these generations. Here, among the many "begats," is the brief biography of a man named Jabez and his remarkable prayer for prosperity and power:

> And Jabez was more honorable than his brethren; and his mother called his name Jabez, saying, "Because I bare him with sorrow." And Jabez called upon the God of Israel saying, "Oh that Thou wouldest bless me indeed, and enlarge my coast, and that Thine hand might be with me, and that Thou wouldest keep me from evil that it may not grieve me!" And God granted him that which he requested (1 Chron. 4:9-10).

## PRAYING HYDE

The prayer of Jabez moved the heart of missionary John Hyde to pray with great faith, expecting answers to his prayers. As a result, he became known as Praying Hyde and the world still feels the impact of his powerful life.

Dr. J. Wilbur Chapman once wrote to a friend, telling of

Praying Hyde's influence on him. He had been holding meetings in England, but the attendance had been disappointingly small. Then he received word that Praying Hyde was going to pray down God's blessing upon him and his work.

As a result of Hyde's powerful praying, the tide soon turned and the meeting hall became packed with people. At Chapman's first public invitation, fifty men received Christ as their Saviour. Relating the story, Chapman said:

> As we were leaving I said, "Mr. Hyde, I want you to pray for me." He came to my room, turned the key in the door, and dropped to his knees, and waited five minutes without a single syllable coming from his lips. I could hear my own heart thumping, and his beating. I felt hot tears running down my face. I knew I was with God. Then with upturned face, down which the tears were streaming, he said, "0 God." Then for five minutes at least he was still again; and then, when he knew that he was talking with God, there came from the depths of his heart such petitions for me as I nad never heard before. I rose from my knees to know what real prayer was."[1]

Chapman's belief in the power of prayer was stronger than ever before after that meeting with the man whose own heart had been set on fire by the prayer of Jabez. He never forgot that wonderful encounter with Praying Hyde.

## REACHING OUT FOR GOD'S BEST

Jabez was evidently a man who could not be satisfied with less than God's best. Some may plod on year after year accomplishing little but not Jabez; he had to have all that it was possible for him to claim. No spiritual ruts for him. He insisted on doing more in life than just marking time. He asked God to enlarge his territory. And God granted his request.

Caleb was also such a man. Like Joshua, he had been chosen by Moses to be one of the twelve spies sent into Canaan to scout the land. He had returned with full confidence that in God's power the Israelites could conquer the land and enjoy its bounty. But he and Joshua were in the minority in presenting this view and their report was rejected. The other spies had been intimidated by the size of the Canaanites and believed an invasion was too risky. Accepting this faithless report kept the Israelites confined to the wilderness, preventing them from enlarging their territory and possessing the Promised Land.

Forty years later, after an entire generation had died except for Caleb and Joshua and their families, the Children of Israel crossed the Jordan River and set out to conquer Canaan. Caleb was now eighty-five years old but his courage was strong. Declaring that he was as able to make war now as in his youth, this courageous senior citizen asked for the toughest part of Canaan to conquer. He wanted to engage the giants of the land in battle, the very warriors who had frightened his fellow spies so badly forty years earlier. "Now therefore give me this mountain," he cried. And that mountain was the stronghold of the most powerful fighting men in Canaan. His request was granted and after driving out the enemy he triumphantly claimed the mountain for his own (Josh. 14—15).

David had been anointed king over Israel, but Saul still occupied the throne. There seemed little hope that this young former shepherd could replace the king and assume his God-appointed duties. The establishment was against him and they had most of the manpower and weapons. David's followers were a sorry lot in the eyes of most people; they were a company of discontents and outcasts, described as follows: "And everyone that was in distress, and every one that was in debt, and everyone that was discontented gathered themselves unto him; and he became a captain over them; and there were with him about 400 men" (1 Sam. 22:2).

The military prospects for David and his men were not good. Yet God would develop mighty men out of this ragtag army, and David would expand his control over the land until one day he would finally become king.

We do not have to settle for less than God's best. We can have more than we have now. Greater spiritual victories await us than we have known in the past. We do not have to live in defeat. The power of sin can be broken. Temptation can be overcome. Fears can be conquered; anxieties put away. Depression can be but a memory. We should not expect to be losers because we are equipped to win.

## THE BELIEVER'S BLESSINGS

As believers in Christ, we have come into full favor with God. In Paul's words, we have been blessed with all spiritual blessings in heavenly places in Christ (Eph. 1:3) and are now "accepted in the beloved" (Eph. 1:6). We are now the children of God and can expect that He will enable us to make whatever changes are necessary to accomplish His will and enjoy the abundant life.

If you are tired of the rut you are in, God will help you get out of it. If you feel that you have been marking time long enough and are serious about getting on the move for God, He can move circumstances and provide the direction you need to get in motion, heading you toward your chosen goal.

You can enlarge your territory, increase your outreach, and extend your influence. God will make it possible. But you must to cooperate with Him if all these good things are to become real in your life.

## VISION IS VITAL

In order to enlarge your territory, you need a clear vision. That is, you need to believe that God is going to do great things for and through you. Vision is related to faith in that it enables one to see faith's work finished before it begins.

Vision sees a building constructed before the plans are drawn. Vision sees a prospering business before the first sale is made. Vision sees a family united when it is still torn by strife. Vision sees a church burning with concern for lost people in the community while dead formalism still holds the congregation in its cold, icy grip.

Ask God for vision. If you do not have vision, there will be no hope of success. Solomon wrote: "Where there is no vision, the people perish" (Prov. 29:18).

Early in my ministry, I had difficulty getting a good attendance at the Sunday evening service. The morning crowds were encouraging and steadily increasing, but Sunday evening was a different story. Week after week, I ministered to a disappointing number of people on Sunday evening.

Unfortunately, most of my fellow ministers were having the same problem and therefore were of little help. When I discussed my frustrations with them, they said they could understand my discouragement but that the situation was general in most churches and that there wasn't much that could be done about it. This made me feel a bit better since it relieved me of the sense of failure. True, I was not succeeding but neither were my friends. It was easy then to conclude that such Sunday night apathy among Christians was just a sign of the times and something to be expected.

Then I met a pastor who turned everything around. We had taken our youth group to a large Saturday night rally in a neighboring city. During the meeting, one of our young children began to cry, so I took her out into the foyer of the auditorium and walked with her while my wife remained in the meeting with our other child. Out there in the foyer, I met another pastor, and after getting acquainted, I asked him one of my favorite questions: "How's your Sunday evening service?"

"Great!" he replied. "We have more out on Sunday night than on Sunday morning."

I couldn't believe what I was hearing.

"How do you do it?" I asked.

"Well, for one thing, I preach all of my best sermons on Sunday night," he answered. "Last Sunday night I preached on 'The Mayor's Wife' and we were packed." Actually, the text of his sermon had been Luke 17:32: "Remember Lot's wife." But he had the crowd intrigued and they were out in force to hear him.

I went home from that meeting a different man. This new friend had convinced me that great Sunday evening services are still possible. While others had bemoaned the competition of television and the signs of the times, he had urged me to give my best to preparation and preaching and not to give in to discouragement.

The next morning, I told my congregation about the encounter with this fiery preacher and declared that we were through having small Sunday evening services. I knew now that our church building could be packed on Sunday evening, and I set out to do my part to make that happen.

One of the members of the congregation asked if a preservice prayer meeting might be started in which we could pray for the power of God upon the Sunday evening service. I was delighted with the idea, and before long we were having more people in the preservice prayer meeting than had formerly attended the service itself.

As the weeks went by, the number of people attending church on Sunday evening kept increasing. Finally, it was the expected thing to have a packed building on Sunday night. Many came to Christ in those Sunday evening services, and a number of them are now in the ministry or some other full-time Christian work.

What caused this change? Vision.

As long as I was discouraged about our Sunday evening service and not really expecting an improvement, the interest and attendance lived up to my expectations. That meeting with the pastor who believed big changed my view of what could happen, and I began to see the church full even before that really took place. Once I could visualize the crowds coming, we were on our way to reaching that goal.

Every great accomplishment is born in vision. Michelangelo stood before a rough block of marble studying it. After a time of silence, he said, "There is an angel in that block and I am going to liberate him!"

One with lesser vision could not have seen the marble angel. What can you liberate? Would you like to liberate success? Expanded outreach? You will never set any of these free in your life until you can envision their release. When vision comes, it will give birth to dynamic faith. And when faith gets active you are in the mountain moving business.

## THE POWER OF FAITH

Faith dares to move ahead, building vision into reality. Doubt cringes and cowers. Faith is bold, expecting God to open doors and give strength for any task.

In his challenging book *Paths to Power*, A.W. Tozer contrasts two kinds of life: dynamic and static. He sees the dynamic periods as those times when believers have marched forward in faith, fearlessly carrying God's message to the world. During these times, he says, these faithful ones have exchanged the safety of inaction for the hazards of God-inspired progress and points out that God's power has always followed this kind of courage. The static periods, on the other hand, have been those times when God's people have been afraid to advance or have become weary of the struggle and have settled down to conserve their gains. He writes:

> Bible history is replete with examples. Abraham "went out" on his great adventure of faith, and God went with him. Revelations, theophanies, the gift of Palestine, covenants and promises of rich blessings to come were the result. Then Israel went down into Egypt, and the wonders ceased for 400 years. At the end of that time Moses heard the call of God and stepped forth to challenge the oppressor. A whirlwind of power accompanied that challenge, and Israel soon began to march. As long as she dared to march, God sent out His miracles to clear the way before her. Whenever she lay down like a fallow field, He turned off His blessing and waited for her to rise again and command His power.
>
> In every denomination, missionary society, local church or individual Christian this law operates. God works as long as His people live daringly: He ceases when they no longer need His aid.[2]

People of faith have accomplished deeds that have seemed utterly impossible. Imagine how Gideon must have felt when God rejected all but 300 of his army of 32,000 men and then told him that he would be victorious over the Midianites with the few that remained (Jud. 7). And consider how these 300 were armed for battle: each man had a trumpet, a pitcher, and a lamp. Yet this tiny company overcame the enemy by God's power.

Faith brings the impossible within reach because it taps the resources of Almighty God. Doubt imprisons; faith releases. Doubt retreats; faith advances.

## FAITH WORKS FOR PEOPLE OF ALL AGES

When the Rev. Bill Hawks was 64 years old, he accepted a call to be a missionary to Kenya, East Africa. Accepting that call had not been part of his plan. Having completed a long pastoral ministry, he intended to retire. Upon returning to his home in St. Joseph, Missouri after teaching in a Bible conference for youth, however, he discovered a letter in his mail from the secretary of his denominational mission board saying that missionaries were urgently needed in three areas: Singapore, India, and Nairobi, Kenya. Right there on the porch of his home, he said, "But, Lord, I'm too far along—too old to go to the mission field." Then he remembered that Moses had been 80 years old when he was called to active duty and that Noah had been 480 when he started building the ark.

After a considerable amount of prayer, Bill told the mission board secretary that he felt the Lord was calling him to go to one of the places named in the letter. By then, others had been chosen to go to Singapore and India, so plans were made for him to go to Kenya to establish a Bible college.

While flying to Kenya, Bill busied himself reading *The New York Times* and found an article about the country to which he was headed. The article added a new dimension to the venture, telling of a Communist threat there that was centered in a large new building complex known as Lumumba that had been built to house a college. Bill hadn't thought about that possible danger and was somewhat disturbed by the news. When he arrived in Kenya, he was even more concerned. He learned that the location of the Bible college was to be across the street from Lumumba.

Believing that God had called him to Kenya and would therefore protect him and enable him to establish the school on this property, he began praying earnestly that God would take care of the problem. This calmed his fears and increased the feel of adventure in this African mission.

Before long, the Communists made their move. Thinking

they were strong enough to start a revolt, they captured the local radio station and started broadcasting their call to others to join them. But they had underestimated the power of the government forces and were quickly overcome by them.

At Lumumba, however, the Communist activity continued. Setting up loudspeakers across from the Bible college, they blared out their message loudly for forty days and nights.

Bill and his associates went to prayer over this trial, claiming God's promises in the Bible and asking Him to end the disturbance and close Lumumba.

Finally, others in the area protested to the police about the constant noise and the Communists were silenced. They were then driven from the area and Lumumba's fine new buildings evacuated. The Bible college could now be developed.

But there is more.

During their second term of missionary service in Kenya, Dr. and Mrs. Bill Hawks saw the excellent facilities of Lumumba, that had been standing empty, made available to the Bible college to use for their Sunday services and graduation exercises. God had delivered them from their trial and in doing so had enlarged their territory. They praised the Lord for His goodness and mercy.

## THE IMPORTANCE OF WORK

Enlarging your territory will also demand work. Nothing works unless you do. Vision without faith and work makes you only a visionary, dreaming great dreams but never seeing them come to reality. Even mighty faith must be expressed in some kind of action. James wrote: "Even so faith, if it hath not works, is dead, being alone" (James 2:17).

We cannot expect to enlarge our territory without hard work. Dreams take visible form through planning and perspiration.

Those who look with envy at the accomplishments of others often overlook the long hours of labor that were necessary to make these achievements possible. When the grass looks greener on the other side of the fence, it may well be that they take better care of it over there.

In the Book of Proverbs, Solomon made a number of

observations about the high cost of laziness. Consider a few of them:

> He also that is slothful in his work is brother to him that is a great waster (Prov. 18:9).
>
> The sluggard will not plow by reason of the cold; therefore shall he beg in harvest, and have nothing (Prov. 20:4).
>
> Love not sleep, lest thou come to poverty; open thine eyes, and thou shalt be satisfied with bread (Prov. 20:13).
>
> I went by the field of the slothful, and by the vineyard of the man void of understanding; and, lo, it was all grown over with thorns, and nettles had covered the face thereof, and the stone wall thereof was broken down. Then I saw, and considered it well; I looked upon it, and received instruction. Yet a little sleep, a little slumber, a little folding of the hands to sleep, so shall thy poverty come as one that traveleth; and thy want as an armed man (Prov. 24:30-34).

God seems always to call busy people into His service. Moses was tending sheep when he received his call from the burning bush. Elisha was plowing with twelve yoke of oxen when Elijah called him to take his place. Peter, James, and John were fishing when Jesus called them to become fishers of men. Upon responding to the Lord's call, we find new opportunities to labor, discovering that all our work now has an eternal dimension. Perhaps Paul said it best: "And whatsoever ye do, do it heartily as to the Lord, and not unto men, knowing that of the Lord ye shall receive the reward of the inheritance, for ye serve the Lord Christ" (Col. 3:23-24).

Even before the fall of man, it was in the plan of God to fill our lives with meaningful labor. The oldest occupation on earth is farming. God placed Adam in the Garden of Eden and instructed him to dress it and keep it (Gen. 2:15). We should not be surprised then to find that hard work is still required to be successful and to do the will of God.

Fourteen years ago, my wife, Pauline, and I stood in the

center of a large lot in a beautiful setting discussing its purchase with a real-estate broker. "It's a beautiful lot," Pauline said.

I saw the beauty surrounding us, but the lot itself looked pretty bleak to me. With the exception of a narrow ridge atop the hill at its rear, all the topsoil had been stripped from the lot, leaving bare gravel. There was just one tiny maple tree at each corner in the front near the street. Still, my wife said it was beautiful, and knowing that her eye for beauty was sharper than mine, and that the price was right, I agreed it would be wise to make the purchase.

As the years passed, the beauty that Pauline had seen while standing on that barren lot began to appear. But not without a great deal of labor.

After our house was built, many loads of topsoil were trucked in to cover the gravel. Using a tractor equipped with a blade for grading, I shaped and terraced the large yard. My lady with vision developed flower beds and placed trees and shrubs at appropriate places around the property. All helped fulfill her dream of what this drab looking pile of dirt could become.

Recently, I walked over our lot and admired it. During my tour, I counted forty-eight trees and thirty-six shrubs, all seeming to be placed as if they belonged there. Now one of my first joys of the day is a trip to my upstairs study window to view our beautifully landscaped yard and to appreciate the handiwork of God in it all. In the distance, rolling hills provide a scenic frame for the picture we've been developing. But these pleasant surroundings would not have come into being without vision, faith, and work. These are the ingredients of progress and success.

## IMPROVING YOUR LOT

You can enlarge your territory.
Envision success.
Believe big.
Give your best effort to every task.
New opportunities will open for you.
And your lot will keep improving every day.

# THREE
# PRAY LIKE A WINNER

Most of us know that as believers we are equipped to win.

Unfortunately, we lose many important battles because we neglect to use our equipment.

## ELIJAH: PROPHET OF POWER

Elijah was without question one of the greatest of Old Testament prophets, a man of immense courage and faith. Arriving on the scene in a time of national crisis, brought on by marked moral and spiritual decline, he was God's chosen man for the occasion.

We are introduced to Elijah through his unusual weather forecast made to wicked King Ahab: "And Elijah the Tishbite, who was of the inhabitants of Gilead, said unto Ahab, 'As the Lord God of Israel liveth, before whom I stand, there shall not be dew nor rain these years, but according to my word' " (1 Kings 17:1).

The king may have been skeptical of the prophet's warning, but if so his doubts must have been short lived. Drought settled in upon the land and it did not rain in Israel for three and a half years.

During the famine that resulted from the lack of rain, Elijah was a model of patience and faith. First he stayed by the brook Cherith, as had been commanded by the Lord, where he drank of the brook and ate food that was brought to him by ravens. After the brook dried up, he obediently went to Zerephath, where he had been told he would be sustained by a widow.

Upon arriving there, he found the widow about to prepare what she thought would be her last meal. She had but a small amount of meal and oil left. Elijah instructed her to bake a little cake for him first and to use the remainder of her provisions for herself and her son. But then he added this thrilling promise: "The barrel of meal shall not waste, neither shall the cruse of oil fail, until the day that the Lord sendeth rain upon the earth" (1 Kings 17:14). In following the word of God spoken through Elijah, the widow was rewarded: her meager supply was never exhausted, lasting throughout the entire famine.

Later, the widow's son became ill and died. Crying out to God on the widow's behalf, Elijah saw the boy's life return to him. Convinced now of Elijah's relationship to God and his power in prayer, the widow said: "Now by this I know that thou art a man of God, and that the word of the Lord in thy mouth is truth" (1 Kings 17:24).

Elijah's greatest victory was still ahead. Calling together on Mount Carmel the prophets of the false god Baal, he challenged them to a contest. A sacrifice was to be placed upon an altar with no fire under it. First, the prophets of Baal would pray to their god, then Elijah would pray. The coming of fire to consume the sacrifice would prove whether Baal or Elijah's God was to be worshiped.

Baal's prophets agreed to the test and prepared their sacrifice. They prayed loudly from morning until noon, saying: "0 Baal, hear us" (1 Kings 18:26). But no answer came. As the hours wore on, they increased their cries and even began to cut themselves with knives, hoping to impress their god; but it was all to no avail.

After the prophets of Baal had tried to produce fire for their sacrifice without success, Elijah built an altar and made a trench all around it. He then called for twelve barrels of water to be poured over the sacrifice, drenching it and filling the trench. After this had been done, he offered this brief prayer of faith:

Lord God of Abraham, Isaac, and of Israel, let it be
known this day that Thou art God in Israel, and that I
am Thy servant, and that I have done all these things at
Thy word. Hear me, O Lord, hear me, that this people
may know that Thou art the Lord God, and that Thou
hast turned their heart back again (1 Kings 18:36-37).

Immediately the fire fell and consumed the sacrifice and the
wood and licked up the water that was in the trench. The
people watching were convinced, crying out, "The Lord, He
is the God; the Lord, He is the God" (1 Kings 18:39). Elijah
had been vindicated in his bold action, and many turned from
idol worship to serve the Lord.

## ELIJAH'S DOWN DAYS

With such an illustrious past and an even greater future, it
seems a shame to look in on Elijah during a time of depression
and defeat. Yet that is exactly the scene given in the Bible
following his impressive victory on Mount Carmel. There on
the mountain everything had gone his way. After proving
God's power and his position as a prophet, he prayed for rain
and received a cloudburst. The land was refreshed and the
drought ended; the famine was over.

That was when Elijah's trouble began. He received word
from Queen Jezebel that he was to be executed. Elijah's
reaction to this message seems totally inconsistent with his
character. He ran for his life (1 Kings 19).

After fleeing a day's journey into the wilderness, he sat
down under a juniper tree and longed to die. Depression
moved in on him, and he thought there was no use going on.
"It is enough," he said (1 Kings 19:4). Mighty Elijah was
ready to give up.

Finally falling asleep, he was awakened by the touch of an
angel who had been sent to encourage him. He looked and
saw a cake prepared for him and water for him to drink.
Refreshed by the food and rest, he started running again,
trying to put as much space as possible between himself and
Jezebel's forces. At last he reached Horeb and entered a cave,
believing it was a good place to hide.

It was then that God rebuked Elijah with this question: "What doest thou here, Elijah?" (1 Kings 19:9)

God's man of the hour was in retreat. Like most backsliders, Elijah dodged God's question and began grumbling about the faults of others, saying: "I have been very jealous for the Lord God of hosts, for the Children of Israel have forsaken Thy covenant, thrown down Thine altars, and slain Thy prophets with the sword; and I, even I only, am left, and they seek my life to take it away" (1 Kings (19:10).

What followed must have been more frightening than anything Elijah had ever experienced. A great wind swept through the mountains, breaking rocks in pieces. A powerful earthquake shook the area. Fire broke out on the mountain. Then Elijah heard a still, small voice asking again, "What doest thou here, Elijah?" (1 Kings 19:13)

It was a good question. Why was this powerful prophet in the pits? How could one who had been so strong now be so weak? What had caused God's man of the hour to move from the mountaintop to the valley in such a short time?

There is but one answer: he had stopped trusting in God's power that had been available to him through prayer and had chosen instead to depend upon his own ability to cope with his present crisis. He was therefore as weak as any other man.

This is Elijah, the man who prayed that it would not rain and not a drop fell for three and a half years. This is the prophet who prayed for a dead boy and saw him come to life again. This is the man of God who called down fire from heaven, consuming the sacrifice on Mount Carmel and licking up the water in the trench that completely surrounded the altar.

But we must not forget that he was a man. James called him, "a man of like passions as we are" (James 5:17).

This man who prayed with such great faith was not immune to failure. Nor are we if we neglect to use the spiritual power that is available to us.

Paul has written:

For though we walk in the flesh, we do not war after the flesh. For the weapons of our warfare are not carnal, but

> mighty through God to the pulling down of strong-
> holds, casting down imaginations, and every high thing
> that exalteth itself against the knowledge of God, and
> bringing into captivity every thought to the obedience of
> Christ (2 Cor. 10:3-5).

This is a good description of Elijah acting in the power of
God: prophesying drought, raising the widow's son, and
calling down fire on Mount Carmel. But the moment he
chose to face his problems in his own strength, he failed. Faith
and victory were then replaced by fear and defeat.

## NEGLECTING THE POWER OF PRAYER

What if Elijah had chosen prayer instead of panic upon
receiving Jezebel's threatening message? Could standing up to
the wicked queen have been more difficult than bringing life
back into the widow's son or calling fire from heaven to
consume the drenched sacrifice?

Why then do we neglect prayer? Certainly not because we
lack encouragement from our Lord to pray. In his powerful
book *Getting Things from God*, Charles Blanchard wrote:

> In all the record of His dealings with men, there is not
> one instance in which He found fault with men for
> coming too frequently, for asking too largely. On the
> other hand, He at times reproved men because they
> asked too little or because they did not persevere. The
> whole spirit of His directions is, "Open thy mouth wide,
> and I will fill it" (Ps. 81:10). Is it not remarkable that
> men have to be urged, argued with, entreated to appro-
> priate an opportunity of this kind?[1]

## INVITATIONS TO PRAY

Consider just a few of the many invitations to pray . . . and
win . . . given in the Bible:

> Call unto Me, and I will answer thee, and show thee
> great and mighty things, which thou knowest not (Jer.
> 33:3).

Ask, and it shall be given you; seek, and ye shall find; knock, and it shall be opened unto you (Matt. 7:7).

Therefore I say unto you, What things soever ye desire, when ye pray, believe that ye receive them, and ye shall have them (Mark 11:24).

Hitherto have ye asked nothing in My name: ask, and ye shall receive, that your joy may be full (John 16:24).

## EXAMPLES OF ANSWERED PRAYER

And does God answer prayer?

Ask David, who wrote: "This poor man cried, and the Lord heard him, and saved him out of all his troubles" (Ps. 34:6).

Ask Daniel, who spent a night with a den full of hungry lions and lived to tell about it (Dan. 6).

Ask Jonah, who cried out to God from inside the great fish and soon found himself on dry ground, being commissioned again to serve his Lord (Jonah 2-3).

Ask Peter, who was delivered from prison by an angel in answer to the prayers of the early church (Acts 12).

But we must be careful not to limit the power of prayer to Bible times. Prayer is the key to winning in every area of life—today.

Prayer can bring victory to losers; success to those who would otherwise fail. It makes cowards courageous and can bring high hopes to those given to depression.

Prayer produces results—because God is alive.

I can identify with Elijah's prayer for dry weather. For eleven years I conducted outdoor drive-in church services on Sunday nights from Memorial Day through Labor Day. These outdoor meetings were our regular Sunday evening services at the Calvary Bible Church of Benton Harbor, Michigan, where I was the pastor. They were extremely successful and always changed a summer slump period to a time of renewed interest and increased attendance.

There was one threat to our outdoor ministry: RAIN. Showers could force us to move our service indoors, slashing attendance in half. Naturally we prayed for good weather every Sunday night. And God answered.

I can remember only two canceled outdoor services because of rain in eleven summers. Time and again, rain would come on Sunday and continue until it was nearly time to start the drive-in church service. It would then stop and start again minutes after the service ended.

Evangelist Jack Van Impe remembers a similar experience. During his area-wide crusade in Pontiac, Michigan severe storms threatened to force the moving of the final service from a football stadium to a church, a move that would have made it impossible for thousands to attend. A call for prayer went out and the all day rain stopped just before the service was to begin. At 8 P.M., sprinkles began, and the people in the stadium paused to pray. The rain stopped in the immediate area of the stadium, and the service continued. Dr. Van Impe says: "Everything was drenched except one square block of the city."[2]

## PRAYING FOR RAIN IN WEST TEXAS

In his book *Prayer—Asking and Receiving,* Dr. John R. Rice tells of going to hold services in the First Baptist Church of Peacock, a little town in west Texas in 1931. The town was in the clutches of a terrible drought. Crops were almost gone and cattle were dying as a result of water holes drying up. Feeling that God wanted to show His power, Rice promised his Lord that as soon as the people began to show signs of concern over their sins and the salvation of lost loved ones, he would call a meeting of confession and prayer, asking God to send rain as well as revival.

He writes:

> God's Holy Spirit took hold of the people; and they began to have broken hearts, to seek God and to want souls saved. I took courage and called a meeting for prayer, telling the people I felt definitely led to pray for a rain. I felt that the Holy Spirit had put the matter in my heart. Many agreed to pray with me. We publicly asked God to send a great rain and to send it in twenty-four hours. I announced to the public that we would expect a rain in twenty-four hours and that if it came after that

time it would not be the one we were asking for and that we would not count our prayers answered.[3]

The next day the sun beat down fiercely as before. There was no sign of rain. Some scoffed at the young preacher's calling of a prayer meeting for rain, saying that might work in east Texas but not in west Texas where it was so very dry. But at 2 o'clock that afternoon black clouds began to roll in accompanied by high winds. The plate glass windows of a store in town were blown in, and the tabernacle where the meetings were being held was blown off its foundation. There was a great downpour in the town and for about five miles in each direction. Many were moved by this clear answer to prayer and that night packed the meeting, which had to be held in the Methodist church because of the damage done to the tabernacle by the storm. God had honored the prayers of His people, making them winners in the eyes of the community and increasing their faith.

## MIRACLES IN CHINA

In his book *Sit, Walk, Stand*, Watchman Nee describes a preaching mission to an island off the South China coast. There were seven in the ministering group, including a sixteen-year-old new convert whom he calls Brother Wu.

The island was fairly large, containing about 6,000 homes. Nee had a contact there, an old schoolmate of his who was headmaster of the village school, but he refused to house the group when he discovered they had come to preach the Gospel. Finally, they found lodging with a Chinese herbalist, who became their first convert.

Preaching seemed quite fruitless on the island, and Nee discovered it was because of the dedication of the people there to an idol they called Ta-wang. They were convinced of his power because on the day of his festival and parade each year the weather was always near perfect.

"When is the procession this year?" young Wu asked a group that had gathered to hear them preach.

"It is fixed for January 11th at 8 in the morning," was the reply.

"Then," said the new convert, "I promise you that it will certainly rain on the 11th."

At that there was an outburst of cries from the crowd: "That is enough! We don't want to hear any more preaching. If there is rain on the 11th, then your God is God!"

Watchman Nee had been elsewhere in the village when this confrontation had taken place. Upon being informed about it, he saw that the situation was serious and called the group to prayer.

On the morning of the 11th, there was not a cloud in the sky, but during grace for breakfast, sprinkles began to fall and these were followed by heavy rain.

Worshipers of the idol Ta-wang were so upset that they placed it in a sedan chair and carried it outdoors, hoping this would stop the rain. Then the rain increased. After only a short distance, the carriers of the idol stumbled and fell, dropping the idol and fracturing its jaw and left arm.

A number of young people turned to Christ as a result of the rain coming in answer to prayer, but the elders of the village made divination and said that the wrong day had been chosen. The proper day for the procession, they said, should have been the 14th.

When Nee and his friends heard this, they again went to prayer, asking for rain on the 14th and for clear days for preaching until then. That afternoon the sky cleared and on the good days that followed there were thirty converts. Of the crucial test day, Nee says:

> The 14th broke, another perfect day, and we had good meetings. As the evening approached we met again at the appointed hour. We quietly brought the matter to the Lord's remembrance. Not a minute late, His answer came with torrential rain and floods as before.[4]

The power of the idol over the islanders was broken; the enemy was defeated. Believing prayer had brought a great victory. Conversions followed. And the impact upon the servants of God who had witnessed His power would continue to enrich their Christian service from that time on.

## GOD IS ALIVE

So Elijah's God is alive and able to handle problems large and small.

Poor Elijah. He had forgotten that God not only cares for big problems that affect nations, calling for earth-shaking answers such as the withholding of rain or the sending of storms and earthquakes, but that He also cares about threats and heartaches that come to His people. Forgetting this had sent him fleeing into the wilderness, not wanting to see anyone and hoping he would die. Relegating God to the needs of the nation and omitting His power from daily struggles had driven this once powerful prophet into a valley of despair and had him cowering in a cave, defeated, when he was equipped to win.

## RISING OUT OF DEFEAT

Thankfully, Elijah did not stay long in the agony of defeat. Awakened to his need by God's convicting question ("What doest thou here, Elijah?"), he departed his hiding place and returned to his important work.

His successor, Elisha, must be appointed (1 Kings 19:19-21).

He must again face up to Ahab and declare God's judgment upon him and the wicked queen, Jezebel, who had threatened to take the prophet's life, sending him into a period of irrational anxiety (1 Kings 21:17-29).

Elijah would not only outlive Jezebel but would be one of only two men in history to escape physical death. The man who had been so depressed that he had longed to die was taken to heaven by a whirlwind (2 Kings 2:11).

Too many follow Elijah's example given during his down days. Instead of praying in faith about their difficulties, they choose to pout, complain, and give in to depression. They act as if God is dead or that He just doesn't care.

How sad.

They are losers ... when believing prayer would enable them to win.

# FOUR
# TALK LIKE A WINNER

For many months we had been looking forward to the coming of Evangelist Richard Neale of the Youth Gospel Crusade in Westboro, Wisconsin to hold a series of children's meetings at our church.

But shortly before the meetings were to begin, I discovered there was a week-long event going on in the community on the very dates of our coming meetings that seemed sure to drastically reduce attendance. Concerned, I called our evangelist and told him of the conflict. His response to my panic has been unforgettable.

"Well," he said, "in every problem faith sees an opportunity, and in every opportunity, doubt sees a problem." Those wise words were sufficient chastening for my weak faith, and I agreed that we should go ahead with our plans and leave the matter entirely in God's hands.

The meetings were well attended and apparently were not even affected by the feared competition. During that week, forty-one children professed Christ as Saviour. And their pastor learned an important lesson: our expectations need not be affected by negative circumstances. We can expect success even when conventional indicators predict we will fall flat on our faces.

Defeat stalks those who expect it.

Victory comes to those who expect to win.

## THE SOURCE OF WISDOM

One of the reasons believers can be optimistic in their thinking is that they have a ready source of wisdom. James writes: "If any of you lack wisdom, let him ask of God, that giveth to all men liberally, and upbraideth not; and it shall be given him" (James 1:5).

Think of it. We are invited to come to our Lord and receive wisdom to handle any situation. But this promise is conditional. If we come seeking wisdom from the Lord but doubting His answer to our prayers, the desired wisdom will not be given: "But let him ask in faith, nothing wavering. For he that wavereth is like a wave of the sea driven with the wind and tossed. For let not that man think that he shall receive anything of the Lord" (James 1:6-7).

It is impossible to pray in faith while thinking negatively. James calls this being double minded and concludes that double-minded people are unstable in all their ways (James 1:8).

Those who think like winners consider everything in a divine dimension. Their strength may be limited, but they understand that God's power is unlimited. Their abilities may be few, but they know that their Lord can do all things. They expect His power to make the difference between success and failure.

## FEEDING 5,000 HUNGRY PEOPLE

The feeding of the 5,000 is one of the most familiar of New Testament miracles (John 6:1-14). Besides Jesus and the hungry crowd, there are three people who played important roles in the biblical account of the miracle: Philip, Andrew, and the little boy who gave his lunch to the Lord. These three are good examples of those who think like losers and winners.

## PROVING PHILIP

Seeing the multitude coming to Him, Jesus asked Philip: "Whence shall we buy bread, that these may eat?"

The Lord faced Philip with the problem of providing daily bread, a problem that concerns us all throughout our lives. But it is important to note that Jesus saw the problem before he asked Philip to solve it. Nothing takes our Lord by surprise.

How comforting this truth is when we are confronted by trouble!

But there is more good news.

The question was asked for a special purpose: to prove, or test, Philip (John 6:6).

There is a design in every difficulty that comes to a Christian. Philip was to fail the test but would gain experience through it that would make him a better man.

Philip's answer to the Lord's question reveals why it was asked: "Two hundred pennyworth of bread is not sufficient for them, that every one of them may take a little" (John 6:7).

He was thinking like a loser: planning for the very least. If the Lord had followed Philip's feeding formula, each one of the 5,000 would have had but a crust of bread. Philip needed this kind of challenge to his feeble faith. And too many of us are like him. Because of our inability to trust God to do big things, we settle for less than God's best.

What caused Philip to think so small?

He focused on the problem at hand instead of considering the power of Christ to solve it. Concentrating on money and figuring out how far it would stretch limited his horizons.

How strange that this disciple should count only on the money on hand to feed the people when the Lord was standing there beside him! Already, Jesus had performed sufficient miracles to bring religious leader Nicodemas to him seeking spiritual truth (John 3:1-2). At the marriage feast in Cana, He had turned water into wine (John 2:1-11). After that He had healed a nobleman's son (John 4:46-53) and restored health to a man at the pool of Bethesda who had been infirmed for thirty-eight years. How was it that Philip faced this problem without considering the Lord's power?

## THE PROBLEM-CONSCIOUS CHURCH

A church congregation once sent their pastor to me for counsel. There was a serious division in the church, and the people seemed unable to put away their differences.

The troubled pastor explained the situation to me, saying

he couldn't figure out why they were unable to solve their problems. He had been preaching regularly about problems and how to solve them. Following their midweek service, the church board had been meeting weekly to try to solve their problems. The monthly congregational business meeting had been given to airing their problems for a number of months. Still the problems remained.

"Has the Lord done anything good for you?" I asked.

The pastor answered that a girl in her teens had received Christ as her Saviour a few weeks previous to our meeting.

"Then I can tell you what to do," I replied.

"First, stop talking about your problems all the time."

"Second, start rejoicing over the salvation of the teenage girl."

What was I trying to do?

I was attempting to get the members of that church out of their rut of negative thinking. Everything seemed wrong because failure and conflict occupied their minds continually. While they kept seeking for answers, they really didn't expect to find them. They were thinking like losers.

They needed a victory to turn their thinking around—to rearrange their thought patterns. And the Lord had given them just such a victory in the conversion of the girl a few weeks ago.

Somehow, they had missed it.

Compare the atmosphere of heaven to that of the troubled church. Upon the conversion of the girl, heaven rejoiced (Luke 15:7). Meanwhile, back on Planet Earth, the members of her church were momentarily pleased at what had happened but almost immediately went back to feuding. They now needed to return in thought to the miracle that had taken place among them—and to begin expecting God's power to be evident in their church.

Expectation. What a good word it is!

Now consider this: We can expect the *power of Christ* to be operative in our lives and our churches because this is the promise of the risen Christ that is given in His Great Commission: "All power is given unto Me in heaven and in earth. Go ye therefore, and teach all nations, baptizing them in the name of the Father, and the Son, and the Holy Ghost, teaching them to observe all things whatsoever I have commanded you; and, lo, I am with you alway, even unto the end of the world" (Matt. 28:18-20).

After I spoke in a certain troubled church, a woman came to me and said: "I see that you have turned our minds from our problems to the Problem Solver."

That was exactly what I had intended to do. And why not?

We have a victorious Lord who wants to share His victory with us every day of our lives: "But thanks be to God, who giveth us the victory through our Lord Jesus Christ. Therefore, my beloved brethren, be ye steadfast, unmovable, always abounding in the work of the Lord, forasmuch as ye know that your labor is not in vain in the Lord" (1 Cor. 15:57-58).

## ANDREW: THE FINDER

Andrew, the second person involved in the miracle, took a different approach to the problem than Philip. He went out looking for a possible solution.

While Philip was fretting over pennies, Andrew was out finding a possibility. Our first introduction to Andrew reveals that he was a finder. Shortly after starting to follow Christ, he went looking for his brother to bring him the good news that the Messiah had come. John writes: "One of the two which heard John speak, and followed him, was Andrew, Simon Peter's brother. He first *findeth* his own brother Simon, and saith unto him, We have found the Messiah, which is, interpreted, the Christ. And he brought him to Jesus" (John 1:40-42).

The Lord is looking for finders. Every church needs more finders. Finders refuse to settle for the least. They believe there is a solution to every problem and that they have a responsibility to do their part in finding it.

But their greatest value is in their concern for other people. You may find them busy in the community, reaching out to those who need Christ and ministering to those who are hurting.

Finders are encouraged by the smallest gain. Their faith is ignited by even a tiny spark. Like Elijah, who needed only a cloud the size of a man's hand to assure him of a cloudburst (1 Kings 18:44-45), finders see total victory ahead when they prevail in any minor skirmish—because they expect to win.

Andrew searched through the hungry crowd and found a small boy who had brought his lunch. He had very little, but it was all the food that could be found among the 5,000 gathered there. Some might have thought this an insignificant find, but Andrew reported it to the Lord. As a result, the multitude would be fed.

## VICTORY THROUGH SURRENDER

The unnamed boy who gave his lunch to the Lord thought like a winner. He surrendered all he had, believing the Lord would take care of him. But he may not have arrived at that frame of mind immediately. For most, there is a struggle that precedes surrender.

Imagine the scene.

Here is Andrew, a grown man, standing before this boy, the only person among the 5,000 who has any food. The crowd is hungry but so is he. Little boys are hungrier than anybody.

"I'd like to have your lunch," says Andrew.

"Sure you would," replies the boy, "so would everyone else."

"But I don't want the lunch for myself." Andrew explains. "It's for Jesus."

That makes a difference. But the struggle may have continued temporarily. Human nature loves to cling to its possessions.

Then suddenly the battle is over. Young hands hold out the lunch to Andrew. The boy feels relief as he watches Andrew take the lunch to Jesus. And in that act, he has begun to think like a winner. He dares to place all he has in the hands of his Lord, believing he cannot lose. Though he certainly would not have understood all its implications, he has set in motion the law of losing and gaining that would later be explained by Jesus: "For whosoever will save his life shall lose it, and whosoever will lose his life for My sake shall find it" (Matt. 16:25).

## NOTHING TO LOSE

It is totally inconsistent for those who have surrendered their lives to Jesus to think like losers. Everything they own belongs to their Lord, and they have nothing left to lose. All the events of their lives are then designed for their good: "And we know that all things work together for good to them that love God, to them who are the called according to His purpose" (Rom. 8:28).

From the point of full surrender, Christ guarantees His care and blessings:

> And Jesus answered and said, "Verily I say unto you, There is no man that hath left house, or brethren, or sisters, or father, or mother, or wife, or children, or lands, for My sake, and the Gospel's, but he shall receive an hundredfold now in this time, houses, and brethren, and sisters, and mothers, and children, and lands, with persecutions; and in the world to come eternal life" (Mark 10:29).

## WE CAN'T OUTGIVE GOD

In the book *Hudson Taylor's Spiritual Secret,* it is said that this giant for God felt he had never made a sacrifice. Everything he had given to the Lord had been repaid with more than the original gift.

Before beginning his missionary service in China, Taylor at one time worked for a doctor who instructed him to be sure to let him know when his quarterly salary was due. He determined not to do this, however, and to only ask God to bring the paying of his wages to the doctor's mind. He saw this as an exercise in faith building that would help prepare him for the mission field.

Of this experience, he wrote:

> At one time, as the day drew near for the payment of a quarter's salary, I was as usual much in prayer about it. The time arrived but Dr. Hardey made no allusion to the matter. I continued praying. Days passed on and he did not remember, until at length on settling up my weekly

accounts one Saturday night, I found myself possessed of one remaining coin—a half crown piece (about one dollar). Still, I had hitherto known no lack, and I continued praying.[1]

While Taylor was in this money crunch, a poor man came to him requesting that he go and pray with his wife, who was dying. Both men hurried to the home where the woman was and upon arriving there, the missionary to be was moved by the extreme poverty of this family. Describing the scene, he says:

Up a miserable flight of stairs into a wretched room he led me, and oh, what a sight there presented itself! Four or five children stood about, their sunken cheeks and temples telling unmistakably the story of slow starvation, and lying on a wretched pallet was a poor, exhausted mother, with a tiny infant thirty-six hours old moaning rather than crying at her side.[2]

Hudson Taylor knelt to pray but felt hypocritical. The money in his pocket weighed heavy upon his mind. After stumbling through a prayer, he rose and gave all that he had to the poor family, even though he had nothing left now for food or rent and had promised the Lord that he would not remind his employer to pay him his quarterly salary.

God answered Taylor's prayer and restored the woman to health. But the one who prayed was helped too. He later wrote that he felt his life as a Christian would have been wrecked had he not been willing to give what he had to that destitute family, believing that God would take care of him.

The next morning, when the mail came, Hudson's faith was rewarded. A gift came from an anonymous donor amounting to four times the amount he had given away the night before.

"Praise the Lord," he exclaimed, "400 percent for a twelve hours' investment!" And of this victory he wrote: "Then and there I determined that a bank that could not break should have my savings or earnings as the case might be, a determination I have not yet learned to regret."

The lesson learned by Hudson Taylor was the same as the one taught to a small boy who gave all he had to Jesus that day so long ago. Lunch for one became a feast for 5,000—and then some. After everyone had eaten to the full, there were twelve baskets left over.

All were filled with fish and bread, but this boy's heart must have been full of joy and faith. In believing and surrendering, he had become part of a miracle about which millions have read through the centuries since. Apart from the disciples, he is the only person among that great company that we know anything about. Thinking like a winner gave him a place in history and likely started him on a path of blessing and success.

## DON'T BE A LOSER

What goals have you set for the future?

What battles do you want to win?

Stop thinking like a loser and you will probably reach those goals and win those battles. There is no reason for any believer to live in defeat—because we are equipped to win.

# FIVE

# THINK LIKE A WINNER

The woman in the hospital bed beside which I stood seemed to be near the end of her life. Now in her eighties, she had suffered a severe stroke and was in a deep coma. Her heavy breathing added a sad background rhythm to the scene.

I prayed for her, but with little faith. Everything appeared to be so final. I remember telling the Lord that apart from a miracle I could see no hope for her.

One week later, she came out of the coma. Her first words were, "Praise the Lord!" And that was just like her. During my many pastoral visits to her home before her illness, she was always rejoicing.

A farmer's wife and the mother of a large family, she had come through her share of trials. By the time I became acquainted with her, she was a widow, and one of her sons had lost his life in an accident on the farm. Still, she continued to give thanks to God for His goodness to her. That may have been the secret of her long life.

Not long after coming out of the coma, she was back to her farm home and busy about her work. Visitors there found her as positive and thankful as before her illness. God had granted her more years to serve Him, and she was not surprised. Her additional time provided many opportunities to speak to others of His love.

## BIBLE EXAMPLES

Speaking positively places us in good company. The psalmist wrote:

> I will bless the Lord at all times; His praise shall continually be in my mouth (Ps. 34:1).
> Let my mouth be filled with Thy praise and with Thy honor all the day (Ps. 71:8).
> I will greatly praise the Lord with my mouth; yea, I will praise Him among the multitude (Ps. 109:30).

The Prophet Isaiah said: "I will mention the loving-kindnesses of the Lord, and the praises of the Lord" (Isa. 63:7).

Paul and Silas sang and praised God at midnight even in the dark and dismal prison at Philippi (Acts. 16:25).

In view of such powerful statements and moving examples, we ought to look for opportunities to praise the Lord when the circumstances might cause others to complain.

## PRAISING GOD IN TRIALS

Arriving at the church one morning, I noticed a police car in the parking lot. In the church office, I found an officer filling out a robbery report. The officer told me of the theft of some audio equipment during a break-in the night before.

"Praise the Lord!" I replied.

The officer looked puzzled. I explained to him that everything at the church belonged to the Lord and that there was no need to fret about its loss. Certainly God could have prevented the theft had He willed to do so, and I was confident that He could replace whatever had been taken.

This different reaction to the robbery allowed me to witness to the policeman about my faith in Christ. Had I groaned about the loss and made negative comments about the people involved or the criminal justice system, I would have missed the opportunity to talk to this officer about my Saviour. My reaction then would have been no different than that of an unbeliever. We who claim to have our treasures in heaven should never allow earthly losses to cause us to act like losers.

The Prophet Habakkuk is another who expresses a winning attitude in difficult circumstances, writing:

> Although the fig tree shall not blossom, neither shall fruit be in the vine; the labor of the olive shall fail, and the fields shall yield no meat; the flock shall be cut off from the fold, and there shall be no herd in the stalls; yet I will rejoice in the Lord; I will joy in the God of my salvation (Hab. 3:17-18).

## GOD DELIGHTS TO WORK IN THE DARK

Anyone can talk like a winner when winning. But Christians should be able to take the long look, knowing that their Lord is at work in every circumstance of life and that He will bring the best possible result out of any dark situation. Actually, God specializes in bringing light out of darkness.

Consider creation:

> In the beginning God created the heaven and the earth. And the earth was without form, and void; and darkness was upon the face of the deep. And the Spirit of God moved upon the face of the waters. And God said, "Let there be light," and there was light (Gen. 1:1-3).

The incarnation of Christ is another example of God replacing darkness with light. Jesus came into the world to dispel darkness:

> In Him was life, and the life was the light of men. And the light shineth in darkness, and the darkness comprehended it not (John 1:4-5).

In rejecting Christ, men rejected the light and chose darkness. Jesus said:

> And this is the condemnation, that light is come into the world, and men loved darkness rather than light, because their deeds were evil. For every one that doeth evil hateth the light, neither cometh to the light, lest his

deeds should be reproved. But he that doeth truth cometh to the light, that his deeds may be made manifest, that they are wrought in God (John 3:19-21).

When Christ died on the cross, the world was plunged into darkness for three hours. But three days after his death, He arose, bringing light and life to that dreadful scene.

The greatest example of the power of Christ to dispel darkness is seen in the change He makes in the lives of those who trust in Him. Paul wrote:

Giving thanks unto the Father, who hath made us meet to be partakers of the inheritance of the saints in light; who hath delivered us from the power of darkness, and hath translated us into the kingdom of His dear Son (Col. 1:12-13).

God has solved our most serious problem in providing salvation from sin. Why then should we be overcome by daily cares? No matter how dark the present seems, the future of every believer is bright. This ought to make us praising, positive people.

## POSITIVE ATTITUDES ARE IMPORTANT

In his book *Life Is Tremendous!* Charlie Jones says learning to live begins with developing positive attitudes and inner vision. He then explains that the first step in learning to live is learning to say positive things all the time. He writes:

Perhaps as much as 99 percent of our conversation is negative. Some people can't wait for their mouths to open and expose another negative nugget for all to admire. I'm not talking about tongue-in-cheek flattery or snide gilding of the lily, but downright pessimism. I'm convinced that there is nothing that will brighten the atmosphere of a business, church, or home like an enthusiastic person who offers a few positive words to others.

I believe it is possible to say something positive to everybody about everything all the time if we want to.[1]

## WORDS THAT BLESS OTHERS

This is sound advice because words are powerful. What we say affects others. Our words may make winners or losers out of people we meet today. And that places us all under obligation to be positive in what we say.

Solomon wrote: "Heaviness in the heart of a man maketh it stoop, but a good word maketh it glad" (Prov. 12:25).

I am indebted to many who have shared good words with me when I have needed them. Just when I have been about to head down into the valley, God has sent someone along with a word to lead me on to higher ground. This has happened so many times that I am careful now to listen for positive words from others throughout the day. Since the Holy Spirit indwells all Christians, I try to stay alert to faith builders that He may bring to me through people I meet.

I am ashamed that there have been too many occasions when I have not taken time to give a good word to others when it was in order to do so. How easy it is for us to take one another for granted. Probably the people to whom we express appreciation the least are those closest to us.

A wife keeps her house in order for years and her husband just expects it to be that way. He seldom takes her in his arms to whisper words that let her know he notices her good work.

A husband and father labors hard and provides for his family. Finally, after life is past, the children gather at his funeral to talk about what a good man he was. Probably some of those kind comments would have rebuilt his confidence and recharged his vitality, had they come in time. With a few good words, he might have lived longer.

A family works in the church. Dad serves on the board. Mom teaches and sings in the choir. They are faithful in their places at every opportunity. Then one day they are gone. They've decided to try attending another church. Diagnosis? Discouragement! A good word might have improved their service and kept the fire flaming in their hearts.

Speaking positively both encourages and inspires. Who will be moved to great accomplishments by words that are pessimistic? Paul asked, "If the trumpet give an uncertain sound, who shall prepare himself to the battle?" (1 Cor. 14:8)

Empires have been founded by those who were able to motivate others through their powerful and inspiring speaking. On the other hand, churches and other organizations have been destroyed by negative statements.

## NEGATIVISM IS CONTAGIOUS

A retired businessman told me that he had noticed how damaging a few negative comments could be to a committee that was evaluating people for different levels of employment. He said the first evaluation usually proved to be the most important. If the speaker pointed out something positive about the person being considered, quite often the other committee members would also make positive observations. If the first comment was negative, generally the others that followed were also negative.

## POSITIVE WORDS ARE VITAL TO GOOD LEADERSHIP

As I learned how quickly a church takes on the personality of the pastor, I also realized the importance of being positive in the things I had to say.

If we were launching a radio ministry, starting another branch church or deciding to construct a new building, I knew that I must convey a positive attitude to my congregation. Why should they follow one who had ideas about outreach but was unsure about whether these ideas would succeed or fail? By never allowing thoughts of failure to stay in my mind, I could be sure that I would never talk about them. I believed that God was able to lead us victoriously in any project we attempted, and therefore I could speak about winning without any reservations. As a result, we shared many victories.

At the same time, I was impressed by the destructive power of negative words and therefore made it a rule never to say anything negative about any member of my congregation in the presence of any other member. This does not mean that I refrained from speaking out against sinful practices, but it does mean that I was unwilling to criticize fellow believers in the fellowship. I now feel that this principle is one of the most important I can share in my meetings with other pastors.

Two contrasting statements by men of God that are record-ed in the Bible demonstrate the power of negative and posi-tive words.

### JACOB'S MISTAKE

Just before allowing his youngest son, Benjamin, to accompa-ny his brothers to Egypt to get food to sustain them through the famine that gripped their land, Jacob said: "Me have ye bereaved of my children: Joseph is not, and Simeon is not, and ye will take Benjamin away; all these things are against me" (Gen. 42:36).

Jacob's lament is a downer.

If you dwell on it long enough, you may find yourself becoming pessimistic about life. Yet some choose Jacob's mood, frequently talking as if all things were against them.

Actually, for Christians, the opposite is true. All things are for us:

> What shall we then say to these things? If God be for us, who can be against us? He that spared not His own Son, but delivered Him up for us all, how shall He not with Him also freely give us all things? (Rom. 8:31-32)

Jacob's conclusion was wrong. And it is wrong for any believer to adopt his pessimistic statement as an acceptable view of life. Granted, Jacob had come through some tough times. But, while he did not know it, both Joseph and Simeon were alive. Joseph by then held one of the top positions in Egypt and would provide well for his father in his later years. Instead of all things working against him, they were working to bring him some of the greatest blessings of his life.

### JOB'S GOOD EXAMPLE

Now consider a contrasting statement by Job: "For I know that my Redeemer liveth, and that He shall stand at the latter day upon the earth" (Job 19:25). Then he adds: "But He knoweth the way that I take; when He hath tried me, I shall come forth as gold" (Job. 23:10).

Job has by this time lost his wealth, his family, and his health, but he still insists that God is alive and that better days are ahead. His confidence of coming victory is evident in his words and many have been helped by them.

Job's words lift and encourage; Jacob's words depress.

Since others are affected by what we say, it is important to continually be saying helpful and positive things. We have no more right to engulf people we meet in a cloud of gloom than we do to carelessly pollute their water or air. Poisoning the minds of others with negativism can be harmful to their health.

What we say also affects how we think. Negative thoughts are reinforced by negative words. If you start the day feeling down and verbalize your feelings, they will probably intensify. On the other hand, saying positive things can often break a negative mood. Welcome each morning saying something positive, and you almost assuredly will have a better day.

## WORDS CONFIRM FAITH

Talking like a winner often confirms faith. When approaching Goliath, David said:

> Thou comest to me with a sword and with a spear, and with a shield, but I come to thee in the name of the Lord of hosts, the God of the armies of Israel, whom thou hast defied. This day will the Lord deliver thee into mine hand, and I will smite thee, and take thine head from thee; and I will give the carcasses of the host of the Philistines this day unto the fowls of the air, and to the wild beasts of the earth, that all the earth may know that there is a God in Israel. And all this assembly shall know that the Lord saveth not with sword and spear, for the battle is the Lord's, and He will give you into our hands (1 Sam. 17:45-47).

Goliath's size didn't concern David because his confidence was in the Lord. David's faith enabled him to speak like a winner. In doing so, he tasted victory before the battle was won. Shortly after his bold declaration, he defeated his foe.

When we were children, most of us heard the story of the two train engines trying to get up a steep hill. One engine kept repeating "I don't think I can" and therefore could not make the grade. The other said "I think I can" and chugged to the top.

That childhood story contains life-changing truth. If you keep talking about failing, you will probably fail. If you expect to win and declare your confidence openly, you will be able to scale many of life's heights successfully.

## WHAT IF YOU LOSE?

But what if you talk like a winner and lose a battle? There is that possibility.

Peg Rankin starts her book *Yet Will I Trust Him,* asking three thought provoking questions:

> What do you do when you are desperately wishing for a job promotion and you pray for prosperity but you lose your job instead?
>
> What do you do when you ask God to heal you but you get worse?
>
> What do you do when you agonize in prayer over a loved one in trouble and the loved one is not delivered?[2]

Questions like these may be unwanted, but they must be faced. Does this mean that Christians can pray like winners, think like winners, talk like winners, and still be losers?

Not quite. There is a difference between losing and being a loser, just as there is a difference between failing and being a failure.

## JOSEPH WAS NOT A LOSER

It appeared that Joseph had lost many times, but he was not a loser. Being sold into slavery must have seemed like an irretrievable loss. He was taken from his family and home and lost his freedom. Later, he was falsely accused by Potiphar's wife and imprisoned for a crime he did not commit. That must have been hard to bear. Still, in God's time, he was brought out of prison and ultimately made one of the top men in Egypt. Explaining his experiences to his brothers who had sold him to slave traders, Joseph said:

> Now therefore be not grieved, nor angry with your-
> selves, that ye sold me hither, for God did send me
> before you to preserve life. For these two years hath the
> famine been in the land, and yet there are five years, in
> the which there shall neither be earing nor harvest. And
> God sent me before you to preserve you a posterity in
> the earth, and to save your lives by a great deliverance.
> So now it was not you that sent me hither, but God; and
> He hath made me a father to Pharaoh, and lord of all his
> house, and a ruler throughout all the land of Egypt
> (Gen. 45:5-8).

Above the earthly forces working in Joseph's life was the
sovereignty of God. And this same sovereignty lovingly per-
mits or restrains events and forces in our lives, acting as a
safety net for all believers who pray or long for things that
would not be for their ultimate good.

In answering the questions she has raised at the beginning
of *Yet Will I Trust Him,* Peg Rankin appeals to the great faith
chapter, Hebrews 11, writing:

> Look at the phrases in Hebrews 11 that show triumph:
> "subdued kingdoms, wrought righteousness, obtained
> promises, stopped the mouths of lions, quenched the
> violence of fire, escaped the edge of the sword, out of
> weakness were made strong, waxed valiant in fight,
> turned to flight the armies of the aliens . . . received
> their dead raised to life again" (vv. 33-35). These
> phrases belong to "delivered" Christians.
>
> But there are others who were not so blessed. They are
> the ones who "were tortured . . . had trial of cruel
> mockings and scourgings . . . bonds and imprisonment
> . . . were stoned, they were sawn asunder, were tempted,
> were slain with the sword: they wandered about in
> sheepskins and goatskins; being destitute, afflicted, tor-
> mented" (vv. 35-37). The point to be grasped here is
> that delivered and nondelivered Christians all have the

same Sovereign and Lord. He simply uses their lives in entirely different ways.[3]

## HOW TO PRAY

How shall we then pray? Think? Speak?

After many years of wrestling with these questions, I have settled on the following: Ask God for the most, exercise faith, and talk like a winner. At the same time, understand that you do not always know the will of God about every matter and that His will is always best for you. Be continually yielded to God's will, therefore, and totally receptive to His response to your asking, believing, and speaking.

Some may see this conclusion as a lack of faith, feeling that all prayers are always answered if faith is strong. Instead, it simply recognizes our failure to discern God's will in some matters, causing us to pray incorrectly. Paul wrote: "Likewise the Spirit also helpeth our infirmities, for we know not what we should pray for as we ought; but the Spirit Himself maketh intercession for us with groanings which cannot be uttered" (Rom. 8:26).

John said: "And this is the confidence that we have in Him, that, if we ask anything according to His will, He heareth us: And if we know that He hears us, whatsoever we ask, we know that we have the petitions that we desired of Him" (1 John 5:14-15).

Submitting to the will of God in all things should never dim our expectation. Praying, thinking, and talking like winners are evidences of faith and will result in great personal victories.

## THE SAFETY NET

On those occasions when it appears that we have lost out on something we thought was coming our way, let us thank God for His perfect will. The safety net of His sovereignty may well have kept us from a serious fall.

# SIX
# WINNING OVER TEMPTATION

Some people have become distressed because they experience temptation, feeling guilty over the urge to sin. But temptation is common to all. And there is nothing sinful about being tempted. It is in *yielding* to temptation that we miss out on the best in life.

## YIELDING TO TEMPTATION IS COSTLY

Losing the battle against temptation can cancel many other gains. Before the Flood, Noah became a preacher of righteousness and was spared from the judgment sent upon the world at that time. But his great accomplishment of building the ark was marred by his later use of strong drink, causing his family to suffer severely for generations to come (Gen. 9:20-29).

Moses led the Children of Israel out of Egypt and through the Red Sea to freedom. He endured the complaining and criticism of his people and interceded for them time and again when their destruction seemed imminent. But a temper out of control caused him to disobey the Lord, and he was forbidden to lead Israel into the Promised Land (Num. 20:10-12)

Samson was the strongest man of his time. He had immense potential for helping his people and serving the Lord. Enemies of this powerful man were intimidated by his strength. But lust and evil companions ruined him, bringing weakness, blindness, slavery, and an early death (Jud. 14-16).

David rose from the sheepfold to the throne of Israel. He was called a man after God's own heart and was loved by the majority of his people. Everything was going his way. He was eminently successful, a winner indeed. But his affair with Bathsheba brought him sorrow and tainted his reputation through the ages (2 Sam. 11-12).

Sin brings grief. You cannot sin and win.

## HANDLING TIMES OF YIELDING TO TEMPTATION

When we yield to temptation, there is provision for forgiveness. John wrote: "If we confess our sins, He is faithful and just to forgive us our sins, and to cleanse us from all unrighteousness" (1 John 1:9). This does not mean, however, that we should live in constant defeat, having to confess the same sins over and over again. In confronting temptation, Christians are equipped to win.

## OVERCOMING TEMPTATION

One of the encouraging things taught in the Bible about temptation is its universal sameness. Every temptation that comes our way has been experienced by someone else. The setting may not be exactly the same, but the basics of temptation are unchanging. They are: the lust of the flesh, the lust of the eyes, and the pride of life (1 John 2:15-16).

Consider the temptation of Eve: "And when the woman saw that the tree was good for food, and that it was pleasant to the eyes, and a tree to be desired to make one wise, she took of the fruit thereof, and did eat and gave also unto her husband with her; and he did eat" (Gen. 3:6).

The fruit looked as if it would taste good (the lust of the flesh); it was pleasant to the eyes (the lust of the eyes); it was desired to make one wise (the pride of life). This is not to say that all things that taste and look good or that increase wisdom are sinful. But this fruit had been expressly forbidden by the Lord. These characteristics of it then became the tools of the tempter, causing Eve to fall.

The temptation of Jesus followed this same pattern (Matt.

4:1-11), as have all other temptations through the centuries. God limits our temptations to "such as is common to man." Satan is allowed no untried enticements. The world is permitted no unknown allurements, though in different times these may take different forms. The flesh is granted no cravings unexperienced by others in the past.

The temptations we face then are not new. Others before us have been waging the same battles we fight today. Some have won, and others have lost and suffered the consequences. Why not choose to be among the winners? And make no mistake, there are winners whose examples can be followed.

## LOSERS AND WINNERS

Samson and David fell into sin through lust, but Potiphar's wife was unable to seduce Joseph, even though he knew that resisting could get him into serious trouble (Gen. 39). Elijah ran for his life when threatened by Jezebel (1 Kings 19), but Daniel was steadfast in prayer when facing the lions' den for his faithfulness (Dan. 6). Peter denied his Lord three times just before the Crucifixion because of the pressure of the crowd (John 18), but John stood fearlessly at the cross and accepted the responsibility of caring for Mary when asked to do so by Jesus (John 19). Ananias and Sapphira conspired to keep back part of the price of their property from the early church by lying about the amount they had received through selling it (Acts 5:1-11), but Barnabas sold all of his property and brought the proceeds to the apostles so that this money could be used in the cause of Christ (Acts 4:36-37).

Of course, Jesus is the perfect example to follow when battling temptation. He was tempted as we are, and yet did not once commit sin (Heb. 4:15).

## A SKEPTIC SQUELCHED

Once while ministering as a hospital chaplain, I met a man who wanted nothing to do with the Bible. He resented my effort to tell him about Christ and thought he had the perfect squelch for all ministers.

"I'm going to tell you just what I told a young pastor who came to see me back home," he said. "I reminded him that he had many hypocrites among the members of his church and told him to go get them straightened out before returning to talk to me."

He then described the young pastor's reaction, saying that he had simply turned and walked quietly away.

"Now you'll have to do the same thing," he said, gloating.

"No, you're mistaken," I replied, calmly, "for I've not come to talk to you about the members of my church. I've come to tell you about Jesus, and there is nothing wrong with Him."

This squelched the skeptic. His mood changed and he listened attentively while I read a text from the Bible to him and explained the Gospel. The perfection of Jesus was something he had never considered before. He had been focusing on the imperfections of Christians, and these had provided him with arguments against their message. Now, faced with the truth about the holiness of Christ, he could but listen and agree. His old defense crumbled before the Scriptures telling about our perfect and loving Lord.

## OUR VICTORIOUS SAVIOUR

Since Jesus has entered the arena of temptation and emerged victorious, He is able to understand the battles encountered by those who belong to Him: "For in that He Himself hath suffered being tempted, He is able to succor them that are tempted" (Heb. 2:18).

Are you wrestling with temptation? Jesus has been where you are today and understands. Follow Him into the desert and see Him confront the tempter. As in the Garden of Eden, His first temptation had to do with food. Unlike Eve, however, who was well fed and surrounded by plenty, Jesus had not eaten in forty days and there was no food in sight.

Dr. John R. Rice has written:

> Why did Jesus fast forty days? So that He might be as weak as any man ever would be when tempted. He was as hungry, as frail; the temptation as overpowering as any human being ever faced!
> Was Jesus really tempted? Did He feel the tug and pull

of desire? The answer is that He most certainly was tempted. The Scripture says so. He was hungry, tormentingly, fiercely hungry! His poor stomach gnawed with desire. His weakened body cried out for food, and He doubtless felt all the lightheadedness and perhaps delirium that men who go long days without food feel. Certainly, this was a real and definite temptation, as definite and real as any man ever faced. Jesus never one time gave way to it, but He felt the pull of every other temptation that men are ever tempted with. His body was like our bodies. He put Himself in our place and yet never sinned.[1]

There in that barren place, tempted to change stones into bread (a miracle that was well within His power), Jesus answered the tempter: "It is written, 'Man shall not live by bread alone, but by every word that proceedeth out of the mouth of God' " (Matt. 4:4).

After failing to discredit Jesus by tempting Him with food, Satan turned to an appeal to pride. Taking Him up to the pinnacle of the temple, he urged the Lord to cast Himself down in order to prove that He was the prophesied Saviour (Matt. 4:6).

It is interesting that this temptation appealing to pride took place at the temple. Perhaps this is a warning that religious pride is the easiest to slip into. Let a person gain some important office in the church or receive a great amount of praise for some task in the Lord's work well done and pride becomes a dangerous possibility.

Matthew Henry wrote:

> Satan has no objection to holy places as the scene of his assaults. Let us not in any place, be off our watch. The holy city is the place where he does, with the greatest advantage, tempt men to pride and presumption. All high places are slippery places; advancement in the world makes a man a mark for Satan to shoot his fiery darts at.[2]

But Jesus was not deceived. He answered: "It is written

again, 'Thou shalt not tempt the Lord thy God'" (Matt. 4:7).

Finally, the tempter offered Jesus the kingdoms of the world if He would fall down and worship him.

Perhaps this is your area of struggle. A little compromise here and there could increase your income. Bending your convictions would open new doors for you, make you more popular. The world beckons.

But what would Jesus do? Here is your answer: "Then saith Jesus unto him, 'Get thee hence, Satan, for it is written, "Thou shalt worship the Lord thy God, and Him only shalt thou serve"'" (Matt. 4:10).

## GOD IS FAITHFUL

A young missionary was told by a counselor to expect victory over the temptation that was troubling him because of the faithfulness of God. When he had difficulty accepting this, he was told to get alone from time to time and shout, "God is faithful!" You can win over temptation because God is faithful. Maybe you need a private shouting place.

## THE LIMITS OF TEMPTATION

Since God is faithful, He has limited all the temptations you will ever face to your power to overcome them. No temptation that is beyond your ability to resist will ever be allowed to come your way: "But God is faithful, who will not suffer (allow) you to be tempted above that ye are able" (1 Cor. 10:13).

What a promise!

In order to make such a guarantee, God has to know the limit of your strength. And He does! He has already measured your breaking point and forbids any temptation to go beyond it. Our strengths and weaknesses are well known to Him. The psalmist wrote: "For He knoweth our frame; He remembereth that we are dust" (Ps. 103:14).

Neither trials nor temptations can move beyond the limit placed upon them by our faithful God. Henry Ward Beecher said, "No physician ever weighed out medicine to his patients with half so much care and exactness as God weighs out to us every trial. Not one grain too much does He ever permit to be put in the scale."[3]

In her comforting poem "Solace," Wava Campbell has written:

> God weighs your grief and heartache:
> He has an accurate scale;
> He knows about your burdens
> To every last detail.
> God measures all your trials:
> A perfect rule has He;
> He knows about your problems
> Whatever they may be.
> So come and lay your weary heart
> Upon the Holy One,
> And He will give you perfect rest
> Through Jesus Christ His Son.[4]

## SCOFIELD'S VICTORY OVER TEMPTATION

Dr. C.I. Scofield had been a slave to alcohol before his conversion to Christ. After becoming a Christian, he was still so afraid of entering a bar or club where alcoholic beverages were sold that he would often cross the street rather than pass one, fearing that he might yield to the temptation to drink. No one had told him about the keeping power of Christ.

Then one day he saw a painting of Daniel in the den of lions displayed in a store window. The artist had portrayed Daniel standing with his hands behind him and the lions circling about him as he looked up to answer the king's question about surviving through the night.

The painting set Scofield free from his fears. He saw those lions as his old habits and sins and understood that the God who had shut the mouths of the lions for Daniel could give him victory over any temptation. Finding that God was able to deliver him from his own particular lions brought great hope to his heart and rest to his soul.

## JOB'S TEMPTATION WAS LIMITED

Even troubled Job lived in the circle of God's love. First, Satan was allowed to touch his family and property but was forbidden to afflict Job's body (Job 1:12). Later, Satan was allowed to attack Job's body but could not take his life (Job 2:6). Though Job endured great trials, he stayed faithful to the Lord and was later rewarded for his consistency in the face of such trouble and temptation to rebel against God. Had Job been incapable of standing true, the tempter would not have been allowed as much freedom to afflict him as he was given.

While Job's temptation was severe, his eternal rewards will be greater than his earthly suffering. And this is a biblical principle that we should all remember when assaulted by the tempter. God has all of eternity to reward those who are faithful to Him. Paul wrote: "For I reckon that the sufferings of this present time are not worthy to be compared with the glory which shall be revealed in us" (Rom. 8:18).

In addition to limiting temptation to our ability to resist, God has provided us with overcoming power. The Holy Spirit lives within each of us from the moment we become the children of God through faith in Christ. That is why people who were helpless victims of the tempter before conversion are able to throw off old habits and sins after being born again.

## NEW LIFE

The new birth brings new life. "Therefore if any man be in Christ, he is a new creature: old things are passed away; behold, all things are become new" (2 Cor. 5:17).

In his book *Here's How!* Jack Odell says:

> It used to take about a quart of whiskey a day to keep me going. Now I don't need it. I know personally a couple of dozen other people who used to be in the same boat. Many of them were in far worse shape than I. Now, and in some cases for many years, they just don't need it. I know of the case histories of literally hundreds of others. Same thing. No bottle.
>
> Even more surprising, all of these people are keeping dry (really I think they're being *kept* dry) without any effort. They don't have to grit their teeth and set their jaws. They don't use iron willpower to get past saloons.

They don't promise themselves just twenty-four hours more of sobriety. These people are dry simply because they like it that way. They don't *refrain* from drinking; they just *don't need* to drink.

They've been changed. Transformed. Saved.

And others have been changed who were slaves to selfishness, anger, pride, profanity, lust.[5]

## POWER TO OVERCOME

These transformations are possible because believers do not stand against the tempter alone. They have become partakers of the very nature of God (2 Peter 1:4), and the Spirit of God equips them to win over temptation. The enemy is strong, but he is no match for the Holy Spirit. John explained: "Ye are of God, little children, and have overcome them, because greater is He that is in you, than he that is in the world" (1 John 4:4).

## USING THE BIBLE WHEN TEMPTED

The Bible is also a powerful weapon to use when tempted. To do so is to follow the example of Jesus during His temptation. He repelled each advance of the tempter, saying, "It is written."

The psalmist says the Bible can keep us clean and give daily victory over temptation:

"Wherewithal shall a young man cleanse his way? By taking heed thereto according to Thy word. Thy word have I hid in mine heart, that I might not sin against Thee" (Ps. 119:9, 11).

But the Bible that is merely on the coffee table will not enable you to win over temptation. According to the psalmist, it is the Word of God in our hearts that makes us victorious over sin.

So the Bible must become a part of life. This means reading it daily and applying its truth in real life situations. I find it helpful to write out Bible verses on cards daily to be kept on my desk or carried with me. You may find another method that works better for you. Perhaps you will want to start memorizing verses so that they are in mind when temptation comes. Whatever method you choose, be sure that you are systematically taking the Bible into your mind so that it can find its way to your heart and do its part to enable you to win over temptation.

## THE WAY OF ESCAPE

Finally, look for the way of escape from temptation that God has provided for you. No matter how severe the temptation may be, our Lord has promised a way of escape: "But [He] will with the temptation also make a way to escape that ye may be able to bear it" (1 Cor. 10:13).

Heading down a steep hill, coming into a city, I depressed the brake pedal clear to the floor, and nothing happened. The brakes on my car had gone out. At the bottom of the hill, two lanes of cars were stopped at a traffic light. I pumped the pedal again, but the car just seemed to increase its speed.

Bracing for a crash, I steered the car toward the curb on my right where there was a narrow opening between the cars farthest right and the curb. To my surprise, there was no crash or sound of scraping metal as I zoomed through that narrow corridor. Since there were no cars crossing the intersection at that moment, I roared through unscathed, having avoided what had seemed sure to be a serious accident. I had found a way of escape.

Most major cities have evacuation routes that are to be used in times of emergency. Should a natural disaster strike the city or word come of an impending attack, residents would use these escape routes to flee to safety.

In His great wisdom and love, God has required that every temptation we face be accompanied by a way of escape. These disaster exits may take many forms, but they all offer ways to freedom.

Two women who were tempted to take their lives found the telephone a way of escape. One received a call from a friend just in time to stop her from carrying out her planned suicide. The other used the phone to call for help and through counseling given by a pastor found hope and a desire to live.

Sometimes other people have been God's way of escape. Meeting a Christian friend or remembering the consistent life of another has on occasion been enough to deliver tempted ones to safety.

Often, God has sent one of His servants to one under attack from the tempter. The arrival of another Christian right on time has frequently been just what was needed to keep the tempted one from yielding in despair.

Once when returning home from doing hospital visitation, I felt impressed to drive back into the city and visit a family who had recently started attending the church where I was the pastor. Upon arriving there, I found the wife in tears and the husband sitting with a loaded shotgun across his lap, intending to end his life. After I shared some Bible verses with him and prayed for his special needs, he laid the gun aside and is alive today.

Diversions of various kinds have delivered those who were tempted. Perhaps you remember a time when something unexpected turned your mind from some enticement at the crucial moment to keep you from falling into sin.

## WITHOUT EXCUSE

When it comes to temptation, we are all without excuse. God has limited both the tempter and temptation to what others have endured and to what we can overcome. He is faithful and has equipped us with the power to win every contest. In addition, He has made a way to escape in the event we feel too weak to resist.

Commenting on God's provision for Christians to conquer temptation, Dr. M.R. DeHaan wrote: "And this brings us to the glorious truth of the grace of God, which can enable us to live above the circumstances of life, and not be defeated, but victorious in all that we do. We need not fall short of victory."[6]

The good doctor said it well: when tempted, we can win!

# SEVEN

# *POWER TO FORGIVE*

"I can never forgive him." Those are harsh words. Yet they often seem to be true.

## THE LOSERS

The tragedy of an unforgiving spirit is the number of losers it produces. You lose, because as you harbor that grudge it keeps eating away inside of you, destroying your peace of mind. The object of your bitterness loses your full fellowship. Your church loses the warmth and power that comes when all the members are right with God and one another. You know all this and still feel powerless to forgive.

At the conclusion of a church meeting, a woman came in tears to tell me how negatively her life had been affected by her unwillingness to forgive. Once she had been one of the most active members of her church, giving time and talent to reaching and teaching youth. Then, a few years before our meeting, she had become bitter toward another youth worker. As a result, she had spent two fruitless years. That night she had seen how foolish she had been to carry that grudge.

"Can you forgive her?" I asked.

"I've already done so and have told her about it," she replied. The reconciliation of these two who had been unwilling to forgive was a great victory. But the two years they had lost could never be reclaimed. Readiness to forgive at the time of the offense could have rescued both of them from nearly a thousand days of discomfort and spiritual sterility. That period of harboring ill feelings had taken a heavy toll of both of them.

## FORGIVENESS CAN CHANGE A CHURCH

Bitterness between Christians is probably the greatest thief of power in churches today. The first-century church began with a tiny group of believers who, for the most part, had failed their Lord. Yet these weak ones were able to put aside their differences, forgive one another, and get on with obeying the Great Commission (Matt. 28:18-20). As a result, they shook the world for Christ.

A free flow of forgiveness would revolutionize most churches. Barriers erected long ago would fall. Effort now spent in holding the flock together and catering to different factions within could be given to reaching out to the community and the world. An atmosphere of love would replace the cold formalism that characterizes too many local gatherings of the body of Christ.

Such a miracle of love would fulfill Paul's instructions to the Christians in the Ephesian church: "Let all bitterness, and wrath, and anger, and clamor, and evil speaking, be put away from you with all malice: and be ye kind one to another, tenderhearted, forgiving one another, even as God for Christ's sake hath forgiven you" (Eph. 4:31-32).

Imagine all these negative attitudes: bitterness, wrath, anger, clamor (angry shouting), and evil speaking, being absent from your life, your home, your church. Now think of filling the void with kindness, tenderheartedness, forgiveness.

"Sounds like a dream," you say.

Yes, but this dream can become a reality by simply treating others as God for Christ's sake has treated you.

## FORGIVENESS IS POSSIBLE

"I just can't forgive her," the wounded husband said, still longing to somehow hold his family together.

"No, you can't," I answered, "unless you are willing to forgive as you have been forgiven."

Forgiving others as God for Christ's sake has forgiven you is God's unfailing formula for forgiveness.

Recently, I called on a family who had just moved to our area. Standing at the door, I presented the Gospel to the wife and found her receptive to the message of Christ and His love.

"I'd like to be saved," she said, "but I can't be." Then she explained that, though she would like to become a Christian, she was unwilling to do so unless her husband would join her in this decision. She was sure that he would not do so because he was bitter toward certain family members. In her view there was no hope of reconciliation between her husband and his relatives and therefore no hope for either him or her to be saved.

After assuring her that God could enable her husband to forgive, I prayed for the family and went on my way.

Several months passed before this husband and wife received Christ as Saviour. On the day they were converted, I made no mention of the family problem, nor did they. But within a few weeks after coming to Christ, they went to visit their relatives and were reconciled to them.

How could they forgive now when they could not do so before? What made the difference? The love of Christ that had now become real in their hearts enabled them to forgive as they had been forgiven.

## OUR RESPONSIBILITY TO FORGIVE

Commenting on our forgiveness through Christ and the resulting responsibility to forgive others, H.C.G. Moule wrote:

> It was done in eternity from one viewpoint; it was done at Calvary from another; from yet another, it was done on your personal coming into union with Christ by faith; but from all points of view it was an act toward you of immeasurable and wholly unmerited mercy, which must forever give tone to all your thoughts when you have to consider the duty of forgiving. Yes, it calls you to an "imitation," which shall penetrate to the very springs of life, and shall always find its possibility in the fact of your own salvation.[1]

Receiving Christ as your Saviour then not only made a difference in your relationship with God, it also made a difference in your relationships with others. You became part of the family of God, having brothers and sisters in the faith around the world. One of the most recognizable proofs of the reality of your faith was to be your attitude toward these new-found family members. John wrote:

> We know that we have passed from death unto life, because we love the brethren. He that loveth not his brother abideth in death (1 John 3:14).
> Herein is love, not that we loved God, but that He loved us, and sent His Son to be the propitiation for our sins. Beloved, if God so loved us, we ought also to love one another (1 John 4:10-11).

## POWER TO FORGIVE

Power to forgive comes from being forgiven. And both our own forgiveness and the ability to forgive are the result of God's love.

On one occasion, Peter came to Jesus asking how many times he should forgive a brother who had sinned against him. Seven times seemed sufficient to Peter, but the Lord told him to multiply that number by 70, calling for Peter to forgive 490 times. Actually, Jesus was teaching Peter to forgive an unlimited number of times. One who has forgiven 490 times is in the habit of living in the forgiving way.

## A PARABLE ABOUT FORGIVENESS

Following this lesson on forgiveness for Peter, Jesus told a parable about a king who discovered that one of his trusted servants owed him a great amount of money (10,000 talents). The servant must have held a very high position with the king because his debt would have amounted to more than $9 million in today's money. Since the servant could not pay the debt, the king ordered his family sold so that some payment could be made on this huge obligation. Later, however, the kind king decided to forgive the entire debt. This, of course, pictures the forgiveness of our great debt of sin as a result of God's love and grace.

Upon being forgiven, the servant went out and found one of his fellowservants who owed him a small amount of money (100 pence or about $15) and threatened to have him thrown into prison if he did not pay up immediately (Matt. 18:23-35).

In his book *The Parabolic Teaching of Scripture,* G.H. Lang says of this ungrateful servant:

> Grace did not produce grace, mercy did not beget mercy, forgiveness did not make him forgiving. He accepted mercy but demanded justice. Dealt with in grace he enforced law. Treated tenderly he acted harshly. And it was over a sum so paltry as compared with his own vast debt, merely a few pounds—such is the heaviest liability of my brother to me as contrasted with mine to God.[2]

In this parable, the first principle of forgiveness comes through strongly. We must forgive because we have been forgiven. But another dimension is added: Our debt of sin that has been forgiven far exceeds any debt owed to us by any other person. We have never been wronged to the extent that we have wronged God, yet He has forgiven us. Therefore, we ought to be quick to forgive others.

In *Notes on the Parables,* Richard Trench explains:

> The purpose of this parable is to make clear that when God calls on a member of His kingdom to forgive, He does not call on him to renounce a right, but that he now has no right to exercise in the matter; asking for and accepting forgiveness, he has implicitly pledged himself to show it.[3]

He adds that the small debt owed by the fellowservant to the unmerciful one shows how little one can offend against his brother, compared with the amount in which every man has offended against his God.

## FORGIVE BECAUSE WE HAVE BEEN FORGIVEN

Here then is the foundation for all forgiveness: We have never been wronged to the extent that we have wronged God. Since

He has forgiven us, we can forgive those who have wronged us.

Strangely, the world often recognizes this truth when Christians are blind to it. Let a group of believers be given to strife, and the community will rebuke them for it. In the parable, the onlookers saw the inconsistency of the unmerciful servant and felt bad about it (Matt. 18:31). Jesus said that the world would recognize the power of love working among His followers and know that they were genuine: "By this shall all men know that ye are My disciples, if ye have love one to another" (John 13:35).

## JESUS IS OUR EXAMPLE

The example of Jesus also enables us to forgive. From the beginning of His teaching ministry to His suffering and death on the cross, He was the figure of forgiveness.

The sick, the poor, and the outcasts came to Him for forgiveness, and not one of them was turned away. His openness to the wayward ones fueled fires of hatred among His enemies. They said, "This man receiveth sinners, and eateth with them" (Luke 15:2).

The suffering and death of Jesus declared His forgiveness for all who seek it. When we need to forgive and find it difficult to do so, it is time for a trip to the cross. The first words spoken by Jesus there were, "Father, forgive them; for they know not what they do" (Luke 23:34). Who can hold back forgiveness from others while considering these words from Calvary?

A woman who had been treated wrongly in her church shared her story with me. Though I was sympathetic to her wounds, I knew that her only source of deliverance from self-pity would be a glimpse of her suffering Saviour.

"Has anyone spat upon you yet?" I asked.

"No," she replied, obviously shocked by my question.

"They did on Jesus," I said. And suddenly she saw my point. While she had certainly been mistreated by people who should have known better, she had not endured the pain and shame experienced by Christ in His suffering and death for her sins. My simple question changed her attitude about her persecutions, and she was able to forgive those who had snubbed and avoided her. As a result, she became regular in church services again and was unbothered by the backbiters and troublemakers from that time on. A visit to the cross changed her life.

## THE CROSS DEMANDS FORGIVENESS

Christians who are easily offended and slow to forgive, need to face up to the hypocrisy of this kind of an attitude in the light of Christ's sufferings. How inconsistent it is to say we love and serve the One who endured the cross and then to be so unlike our Lord when called upon to forgive! Actually, in view of Christ's sacrifice for us and the suffering associated with it, we who belong to Him have no right ever to be offended at what others do or say.

## THE CROSS AND HUMAN NATURE

Focusing on the cross gives power to forgive because it reveals how sinful we all can be. In his book *Christ's Seven Last Words from the Cross,* Dr. William McCarrell explained:

> The crucifixion of Jesus, as no other event, reveals the exceeding sinfulness of the human heart, thus of mankind. It brought to light the sin that lies dormant in man's fallen nature. A study of human actions in connection with the crucifixion of Jesus reveals sinful carelessness and indifference to spiritual light, gambling, crime, selfishness, covetousness, cruelty, murder, hardness of heart, unbelief, and rebellion toward God's salvation through Jesus Christ. What sinful curiosity, what shocking mockery of Christ, what foolish defiance and terrible blasphemy of God was manifested![4]

Understanding this, we are better able to prepare ourselves for what people may do to us. Equally important, we grasp more fully the reasons for our own wrong attitudes and actions.

The whole human race is suffering from heart trouble. Jeremiah wrote: "The heart is deceitful above all things, and desperately wicked: who can know it?" (Jer. 17:9)

Jesus said: "For from within, out of the heart of men, proceed evil thoughts, adulteries, fornications, murders, thefts, covetousness, wickedness, deceit, lasciviousness, an evil eye, blasphemy, pride, foolishness: all these evil things come from within, and defile the man" (Mark 7:21-23).

We should not be surprised then at the outward manifestations of these inner urges to sin. Have others treated you badly? Has someone wronged a member of your family? Have you been slandered? Cheated? People have been doing these and more violent things to one another since the fall of man.

Martin Luther called our sinful nature so deep and horrible a corruption of nature that no reason can comprehend it. At the same time, he concluded that it must be believed because the Scriptures declare it. He might have added that experience confirms it. And honest people admit that the problem lies not just in others but in all of us. Augustine wrote: "We are capable of every sin that we have seen our neighbor commit unless God's grace restrains us."[5] Making this admission will cause us to be more ready to forgive, since it reminds us that we have likely wronged others as they have wronged us.

The cross reveals the seriousness of sin and the awful price paid by Christ to redeem us from it. While Handel was composing *The Messiah,* a friend came to visit just as he was working on the music for "He was despised." Handel sobbed as he worked because his heart was so moved by the shame and suffering of Christ described in the text.

Pride is broken at the cross. Calvary is God's breaking place. And broken people cannot long remain bitter over wrongs done to them. They are so grateful for God's love being extended to them that they have no heart for holding grudges against others.

In *The Calvary Road,* Roy Hession says:

> The willingness of Jesus to be broken for us is the all-compelling motive in our being broken too. We see Him, who is in the form of God, counting not equality with God a prize to be grasped at and hung on to, but letting it go for us and taking upon Him the form of a

servant—God's Servant, man's Servant. We see Him willing to have no rights of His own, willing to let men revile Him and not revile again, willing to let men tread on Him and not retaliate or defend Himself. Above all, we see Him broken as He meekly goes to Calvary to become men's scapegoat by bearing their sins in His own body on the cross.[6]

## OUR FORGIVENESS IS UNDESERVED
Entering the store of a Christian businessman, I asked, "How are you today?"

"Better than I deserve," he replied.

His answer should speak for us all. Not one of us is worthy of God's love or of His many blessings. Yet He loves us and showers us with good things. Shouldn't we respond to others in the same way? Can we do less and expect the world to call us Christians? Are these difficult situations that stretch and try us not opportunities to show that our walk with Christ is real?

## GOD'S GRACE ENABLES US TO FORGIVE
Paul saw himself as the least of the apostles because he had once persecuted believers, but he also saw this as an opportunity to show the power of the grace of God that now worked in and through him: "But by the grace of God I am what I am: and His grace which was bestowed upon me was not in vain; but I labored more abundantly than they all; yet not I, but the grace of God which was with me" (1 Cor. 15:10).

Often we limit our thinking about God's grace to that of enabling us to endure trials. But His grace is also sufficient to enable us to forgive when we are wronged. Nothing is more characteristic of the grace of God than forgiveness; the cross is proof of that.

So we can forgive. We can forgive because we have been forgiven. We can forgive because of the example of Jesus in forgiving, especially as was demonstrated on the cross.

## THE HOLY SPIRIT AND FORGIVENESS
And we can forgive because the indwelling Holy Spirit longs to lead us in applying these dynamic truths to every conflict in

life. In yielding to His still, small voice, we will find forgiveness well within our power.

Stop quenching the Holy Spirit when He convicts you about that lingering bitterness.

Stop grieving the Holy Spirit by refusing to forgive.

Allow the Comforter to heal the deep emotional wounds that others have thoughtlessly inflicted upon you—and that you have allowed to remain. Forgiveness heals all such wounds. And you have the power to forgive.

## IN FORGIVING, WE FIND CHRISTIAN JOY AGAIN

A man once came to F.B. Meyer and said that he had lost his Christian joy. He then explained that his misery had begun when his brother had treated him unfairly at the death of their father, bringing a breach between them over their inheritance. At that time he had vowed never to forgive his brother.

Now the brother was going through many trials. His wife and child had died, and he was also near death. The joyless man wanted to go to his dying brother to make peace between them but had promised he would never do so.

"It is better to break a bad vow than to keep it," Meyer said, urging the troubled man to go to his brother while there was still time.

In going and forgiving, he began again to experience joy. Meyer said: "He went, and the smile of God met him there."[7]

Who waits for your forgiveness?

What barriers now exist that ought to be broken down? To whom should you go, declaring that all is forgiven? You can forgive.

Go!

And you will not go alone.

# EIGHT

# WINNING OVER WORRY

John Wesley said that he would just as soon swear as worry. He saw both as acts of unbelief. Yet, many who profess faith in Christ fret over present problems and fear the future. They worry about family members, financial security, health, and a number of other impending disasters. If you are one of these anxious ones, try evaluating your cares.

## WEIGH YOUR WORRIES
Of the things you fear, how many are really likely to happen to you today? If you can feel safe for the remainder of the day, that is enough for now. Jesus said, "Take therefore no thought for the morrow, for the morrow shall take thought for the things of itself. Sufficient unto the day is the evil thereof" (Matt. 6:34).

Which of your concerns tormented you yesterday? Last week? Last year? Have you been down this road before? How many times have you been troubled by the same thought pattern that paralyzes you today, only to find that your expected tragedy never occurred? Can you believe that God will continue to protect you?

What are you worrying about that is so serious it is not covered by one of the promises of God? Exposure to the Bible and its great guarantees builds faith, and when faith comes fear leaves. Isaiah wrote, "Thou wilt keep him in perfect peace, whose mind is stayed on Thee, because he trusteth in Thee" (Isa. 26:3).

Worry is like a rocking chair: it keeps you busy, but you don't go anywhere. It saps your strength, distracts you from important pursuits, and robs you of the joy of living.

## A BIBLE PLAN FOR CONQUERING WORRY

There are three Bible texts that, I believe, are especially effective in overcoming worry: Psalm 37:1-11, Matthew 6:25-34, and Philippians 4:6-8. Out of these rise four principles that can enable you to encounter worry and win. They are:

1. Recognize worry as sin.
2. Remember that God really cares.
3. Refuse to carry burdens that God has offered to bear.
4. Replace worry with positive thoughts and praise.

## THE SIN OF WORRY

A worried woman came to a guest speaker at her church seeking help in handling anxiety. Her distress over a long period of time had taken its toll on her appearance.

"Are you familiar with the first two words of the thirty-seventh psalm?" the speaker asked.

"Yes, they are 'Fret not,' " the troubled woman replied.

"I see that you have only been obeying the first one, 'Fret,' " the wise speaker said. His careful questioning helped the seeker understand that her fretting was an act of disobedience, which is sin.

When John Edmund Haggai, author of *How to Win over Worry,* was twenty-four years of age and the pastor of his first church, he suffered a nervous breakdown. In addition to his pastoral work, he was taking nineteen college hours and conducting evangelistic campaigns. Looking back on that experience, he wrote that the nervous breakdown came as the result of the sin of worry, rather than his heavy workload.

Recognizing worry as a sin started Haggai on the road to recovery. After facing up to his problem and confessing worry as a sin, he overcame his nervous condition. Describing his discovery of the key to his return to health, Haggai wrote:

During those weeks of convalescence God spoke to my heart and showed me that my condition was not the result of any organic difficulty, but the result of the *sin* of worry.[1]

Most are not as honest with themselves as Haggai. Worry itself seems hard enough to bear without having to think of it as sin and therefore be obliged to take responsibility for it. When pressed down by anxiety, it is easier to blame others or circumstances and take the road of self-pity than to face up to wrong doing. Haggai says he also had to wrestle with that aspect of his problem, writing:

My wife felt sorry for me. My church felt sorry for me. My doctor felt sorry for me. But no one felt as sorry for me as I felt for myself.[2]

Tough as it was, however, to acknowledge the truth, Haggai did not get well until he was willing to admit that his worrying was sin. When he did that, he was able to find the way out of his misery by going to the Bible, the only book that reveals sin's antidote.

Defining worry as sin may seem heartless. Instead, it moves this destructive attitude into the area of healing. Once a Christian recognizes worry as sin, the worry falls under the many promises of forgiveness given in the Bible. When worry is excused as just human nature or the result of difficult circumstances, the believer seldom thinks of it as something to be cured by the sacrifice of Christ on the cross. Since worry is sin, the cleansing blood of Jesus can set us free from it: "If we confess our sins, He is faithful and just to forgive us our sins, and to cleanse us from all unrighteousness" (1 John 1:9).

But can we be sure that worrying is sinful?

Absolutely.

Consider the following commands about the sin of worrying:

Fret not thyself because of evildoers, neither be thou envious against the workers of iniquity. Rest in the Lord and wait patiently for Him; fret not thyself because of him who prospereth in his way, because of the man who bringeth wicked devices to pass. Cease from anger, and forsake wrath; fret not thyself in any wise to do evil (Ps. 37:1, 7-8).

Here in the space of three verses are found three commands that forbid fretting (worrying). To worry, then, is to go counter to the clear teaching of the Bible. And that is sinful disobedience.

Worrying is the opposite of exercising faith. George Muller, noted for his life of prayer and faith, said: "The beginning of anxiety is the end of faith. The beginning of true faith is the end of anxiety."

Paul wrote: "Whatsoever is not of faith is sin" (Rom. 14:23). Clearly then, worry is a sin against God because it grows out of doubts that He is really able to take care of us.

## WORRY AFFECTS HEALTH

Worry is also detrimental to our bodies. Fretting drains health away. This makes it difficult to serve the Lord as we ought and limits our usefulness in every area of life. Wise Solomon wrote, "A merry heart doeth good like a medicine, but a broken spirit drieth the bones" (Prov. 17:22).

The American Medical Association recently surveyed several thousand general practitioners, asking: "What percentage of people that you see in a week have needs that you are qualified to treat with your medical skills?" The average answer was ten percent. That means that ninety percent of the people who see general practitioners in America have problems that do not respond to conventional medical treatment. The survey further questioned the doctors as to how they treated these people. Most said they prescribed tranquilizers. In the opinion of these doctors, then, emotional problems are at the root of the majority of complaints brought to them by patients.[3]

Does this mean that these people are not really sick? Not at all. It does mean that our bodies are affected by our mental, emotional, and spiritual states.

A recent report of the Surgeon General says there are indications that stress (generally associated with worry) can be related to vascular disease, gastrointestinal disorders, and mental illness. The late Dr. Hans Selye, an authority on stress, wrote that stress plays some role in the development of every disease.

Since the Bible teaches that the Christian's body is the temple of the Holy Spirit, it follows then that misuse of our bodies is sinful.

## WORRY AND YOUR CHRISTIAN WITNESS

Worry is also a sin against others. Those with whom we have contact have a right to expect us to be living examples of what Christians ought to be. Jesus said, "Let your light so shine before men, that they may see your good works, and glorify your Father, who is in heaven" (Matt. 5:16).

But we cannot glorify our Father in heaven when we are in bondage to worry and the depressed frame of mind it produces. Who will be helped by one who is continually fretting over world conditions or personal circumstances? Why should others be drawn to Christ through our witness if that witness is not backed up by the peace and joy offered by Jesus to those who trust Him? To be effective in serving Christ, our reactions to difficulties must be different from those of the world. C.H. Spurgeon said: "You cannot glorify God better than by a calm and joyous life. Let the world know that you serve a good Master!"[4]

## OPPOSITES OF WORRY

Note also how the psalmist calls for a contrast between the life of worry and the life of faith. While commanding that fretting cease, he writes:

> Trust in the Lord, and do good; so shalt thou dwell in the land, and verily thou shalt be fed. Delight thyself also in the Lord; and He shall give thee the desires of thine heart. Commit thy way unto the Lord; trust also in Him; and He shall bring it to pass. Rest in the Lord, and wait patiently for Him (Ps. 37:3-7).

Repeat these good words again: *trust*, *delight*, *commit*, *rest*. Think about them. Dwell on them. See how different they are from worry and fret.

We owe the world lives that demonstrate what Christ can do in us when we are under pressure. To do less is to miss a great opportunity to benefit others and is a sin against them.

## GOD REALLY CARES

Worry stems from a conscious or subconscious conclusion that things are out of control; that your life has somehow moved beyond the circle of God's love. Like the worried disciples in the storm on the Sea of Galilee (Mark 4:35-41), you have begun to doubt God's care. Of those troubled former fishermen, J.C. Ryle wrote:

> Poor faithless men! What business had they to be afraid? They had seen proof upon proof that all must be well so long as the Bridegroom was with them. They had witnessed repeated examples of His love and kindness toward them, sufficient to convince them that He would never let them come to real harm. But all was forgotten in the present danger. Sense of immediate peril often makes men have a bad memory. Fear is often unable to reason from past experience. They heard the winds. They saw the waves. They felt the cold waters beating over them. They fancied death was close at hand. They could wait no longer in suspense. "Carest Thou not," said they, "that we perish?"[5]

When doubts about God's care begin to move in, it is time to give attention to the life and ministry of Christ. His compassion, His teaching, His suffering, and His death and resurrection all speak of God's care. He had time for all the hurting ones He met and invited the weary to come to Him and find rest. His words were easy to understand, and His lessons were brought home by the use of illustrations about His Heavenly Father's care for birds, flowers, grass, sheep, and other things that His hearers might have thought unimportant to God.

Each morning, I stand looking out my study window while quoting two Bible verses that have become great worry chasers for me:

> Behold the fowls of the air, for they sow not, neither do they reap, nor gather into barns; yet your Heavenly Father feedeth them. Are ye not much better than they? (Matt. 6:26)
> Wherefore, if God so clothe the grass of the field, which today is, and tomorrow is cast into the oven, shall He not much more clothe you, 0 ye of little faith? (Matt. 6:30)

The thought that God cares for the birds that have chosen our backyard for their home reminds me that He also cares for me. Observing the flowers and grass there that go through their yearly cycles and remembering that this is God's handiwork helps me fight off anxiety.

## ONE DAY AT A TIME

The ministry of Jesus also places all events and experiences in perspective, reminding us of God's eternal plan and advising us to take one day at a time (Matt. 6:34).

How important this is!

Think of the cares that would be canceled if we could escape anxiety about tomorrow. Most feel safe about today, but the tomorrows are tough.

Tomorrow the house payment is due. Tomorrow is the final day of grace on the insurance premium. Tomorrow is the day of your appointment with the doctor to find out the results of the test you took last week. Tomorrow is the day you fear that somebody may push the button that will plunge the world into war.

But what if tomorrow does hold unknown trials? Is worry likely to change anything? Ian McClaren wrote: "What does your anxiety do? It does not empty tomorrow of its sorrow, but it empties today of its strength. It does not make you escape evil—it makes you unfit to cope with it if it comes."

The Lord's call to avoid anxiety about tomorrow followed

His instruction about priorities in life today: "But seek ye first the kingdom of God, and His righteousness; and all these things shall be added unto you" (Matt. 6:33).

When Christ is Lord of our lives, having first place in all our thoughts and deeds, we can rest securely in His care.

## LET GOD CARRY YOUR CARES

Most of us have known people who were serene when everything seemed to be crashing down around them. In the most trying of circumstances, they have remained trusting and calm. Those going to comfort them have come away comforted. They have been living examples of the peace of God. The secret of such peace in times of peril is being willing to let God carry our burdens for us. And that is precisely what He has promised to do. Urging his readers to take advantage of this wonderful invitation, Paul wrote: "Be careful [anxious] for nothing, but in everything by prayer and supplication with thanksgiving let your requests be made known unto God. And the peace of God, which passeth all understanding, shall keep your hearts and minds through Christ Jesus" (Phil. 4:6-7).

We will never escape cares. They are part of life. Every circumstance and time of life has its own peculiar set of cares. Therefore we must guard against wishing our lives away, looking forward to times that we think will be less stressful than today.

When our children were young, I often found myself concerned about their health and safety to the point of serious anxiety. Sometimes I looked forward to the time when they would be grown and on their own, thinking I would not be so concerned when they were adults and able to care for themselves. But now that they are grown and have children of their own, I see that the potential for worry is even greater. The tribe has increased, and if I allow myself to do so, I can have a wider worry span than ever. I am just as interested in the health and safety of my children as before and each new grandchild offers another opportunity for anxiety. My concern embraces each family member at birth and challenges my faith. I have learned that I must entrust each new loved one to the Lord or accept each one as another care package.

People who are struggling financially may find money problems on their minds continually. They feel that an increased cash inflow would solve all of their problems. But those with plenty of money also have cares. Surprisingly, most studies show that wealthy people have more trouble with worry and depression than those with less money.

How shall we handle life's cares? Paul's instructions are clear: We are to worry about nothing and pray about everything.

Peter put it this way: "Casting all your care upon Him, for He careth for you" (1 Peter 5:7).

I have a friend who was captured by Nazi forces during World War II. While he was imprisoned, Allied bombing of Nazi territory kept increasing, and the danger of being destroyed by friendly fire became a greater threat than surviving the imprisonment itself. Anxiety over this two-way jeopardy would have been almost unbearable but for a verse in the Psalms that provided strength and hope to him: "Cast thy burden upon the Lord, and He shall sustain thee" (Ps. 55:22).

During the Nazi bombing of London, a Christian woman had such great peace of heart that she amazed her friends. While others found it difficult to sleep, she rested easily. When asked how she could do so, she replied that she had read in the Bible that God never sleeps and that she could see no point in both of them staying awake.

Joseph Scriven, who wrote "What a Friend We Have in Jesus," said we forfeit peace and bear needless pain by not taking everything to God in prayer. That is exactly what we do when we insist on bearing burdens that God has offered to bear for us. In light of this gracious offer, we ought to take our burdens to the Lord and leave them there. When we do so, we can be sure that God is able to take care of them.

## OUR RICH HEAVENLY FATHER

I once worked with a man who had a severe drinking problem. Alcohol had affected his health and finally resulted in a ruptured stomach ulcer that nearly took his life. After being rushed to the hospital, he received a considerable amount of blood and eventually began to recover. His road back to health was hindered, however, by anxiety over debts he had accumulated due to his heavy drinking.

One day, his father-in-law came to the hospital to visit him and while there asked him if he had learned anything from his experience. He answered that he had learned how dangerous it was for him to drink and said that he was through with alcohol.

"If you mean that," his father-in-law said, "I am going to pay every debt you owe and give you a new start."

My friend was nearly speechless at this offer.

"But, Dad," he replied, "you have no idea how much I owe."

"You have no idea how much I have," his father-in-law said assuringly. And after the hospital stay was over, he brought his son-in-law a checkbook of signed checks with which he paid all those debts that had been such a burden to him and that had kept him from enjoying life.

We have a rich Heavenly Father, One who really cares for us. He wants to lift our burdens and carry our cares. He is grieved when we insist on trying to carry them on our own. That is why He invites us to come to Him and find rest. In doing so, we honor Him by our faith and enter into abundant living in Christ.

## REPLACE WORRY WITH POSITIVE THOUGHTS AND PRAISE

Following Paul's revealing of the formula for finding the peace of God, he told the Christians at Phillipi how to keep it. He told them to replace worry with positive thoughts and praise, writing: "Finally, brethren, whatsoever things are true, whatsoever things are honest, whatsoever things are just, whatsoever things are pure, whatsoever things are lovely, whatsoever things are of good report; if there be any virtue, and if there be any praise, think on these things" (Phil. 4:8).

Many take their burdens to the Lord but do not leave them there. Feeling a few hours or days of relief seems almost too much for them. After being without their pity producers for a time, they open their minds to them and welcome them back again. Others are deeply sincere about wanting to be rid of their burdens. They pray and unload, but for reasons they are unable to explain, they find their worries returning not long after praying about them.

Understanding these human tendencies, Paul urged his readers to fill their minds with positive thoughts and praise so that there would be no room for doubts and fears. This principle of victory worked in Paul's time and it works today.

The reason? The mind of man can focus on only one thing at a time.

A woman called recently to tell me how she had won over depression. Victory had come when she busied herself in Christian work. Giving her attention to reaching out to others with the Gospel keeps her from falling into the anxiety and depression trap.

Those who have been given to negative thinking and worrying will have to do some reprogramming of their lives in order to come full circle in this effort, but it can be done. If this is your problem, I suggest that you inventory your intake.

What have you been reading, viewing, hearing? With whom do you fellowship? Are they downers or do they lift you up? Are you positive or negative after being with them? How much time do you spend each day reading the Bible? Meditating on particular verses? Sharing Bible truths with others?

Do you cultivate praise? How much of your praying time is given to praising the Lord? Are you quick to give thanks for things that others take for granted?

My book *Staying Positive in a Negative World* (Victor) should be helpful to you in making this thinking change. Get a copy and give special attention to the chapter on reprogramming.

You can become a positive, praising person. Don't settle for anything less. This will be a vital part of winning over worry, a battle every anxious Christian is equipped to win.

# NINE
# TAMING YOUR TONGUE

Through the centuries, careless and cutting words have wounded hearers and brought regret to those who spoke them. Churches have been divided, family ties broken, and friendships torn asunder by unkind words harshly spoken.

One of the most tragic cases known to me involved a marriage that had suffered a verbal blow shortly after the wedding. The couple stayed together for many years, but the husband never recovered from the bitter words spoken by his bride in those early months of their marriage, and he named those as one of the prime causes of their ultimate divorce.

## THE TONGUE CAN BE DANGEROUS

James called the tongue a fire, a world of iniquity that defiles the whole body and sets on fire the course of nature; and is set on fire of hell (James 3:6). As to the tongue's destructive power, he wrote: "For every kind of beasts, and of birds, and of serpents, and of things in the sea, is tamed, and hath been tamed of mankind: but the tongue can no man tame; it is an unruly evil, full of deadly poison" (James 3:7-8).

In his book *The Tongue—Angel or Demon?* George Sweeting warned:

A fiery tongue is like a burning match in a gasoline tank. The tongue ignites a great fire. A word of hate inflames opposition. A mocking word incites bitterness. An evil word may kindle a career of sin. A foul word heard on the streets, in the shop, in the school, may start fires burning within until nothing is left but ashes.

Contentious tongues have hindered the work of God a thousand times over. Critical tongues have broken the hearts and health of many pastors.[1]

## YOUR MOST SERIOUS PROBLEM?

All of us have spoken words we would like to recall. But an untamed tongue may be *your* most serious problem. Your words or your tone of voice frequently cause you to be misunderstood. You've made enemies when you didn't intend to do so. Others have been offended by things you have said, costing you their friendship. You want to change but have tried so many times before that you wonder if there is any use in attempting to get your tongue under control.

## YOU CAN CONTROL YOUR TONGUE

I have good news for you. Your tongue can be tamed by the Holy Spirit. You do not have to go on being a victim of your own verbal destruction. God can use your words to lift and bless others. You can win over an unruly tongue.

Consider Peter. Before the crucifixion of Christ, Peter was found denying his Lord, cursing and swearing. How he regreted those words! But his carnal and wicked conversation before the cross did not render him useless to God. The same tongue that was used to curse and swear (Matt. 26:74) became God's instrument on the Day of Pentecost to preach to the many gathered there for that occasion, bringing 3,000 of them to faith in Christ (Acts 2).

## THE TONGUE'S THRILLING POSSIBILITIES

The tongue has immense potential for good when it is controlled by the Holy Spirit. A turning point in the life of John Bunyan, author of *Pilgrim's Progress,* came when he heard a few women sitting outside one of their homes talking about the things of God. If they had been gossiping about their neighbors or enjoying some choice morsel of scandal, the effect would have been entirely different. But they were talking about being born again and what a change the work of God had made in their lives, how they were comforted and refreshed by the love of Christ. Bunyan was a tinker, mending pots and pans in the neighborhood, and he said as he went about his work the talk of these good women went with him.

Most of us remember when someone has come along at the right time with just the right words to help us through some difficulty. Later, we had no doubt but that the Lord had sent the person of the hour to minister to our special needs.

Few thrills in life compare with that of knowing you have effectively ministered to another person. Seeing others respond to words you have spoken is a return on your investment that cannot be duplicated. Business gains cannot compare with changed lives.

Pastors stand before congregations and speak words that convict, comfort, and convert. Sunday School teachers and other Christian workers share Bible lessons with children and adults, influencing them for time and eternity. Ministers and other caring people visit those who are sick, hurting emotionally, or imprisoned to speak words that will encourage and build faith. Concerned believers wait for opportunities to tell their friends and relatives about the love of Christ, praying that they will have just the right openings and the right words to bring them to the Saviour.

Solomon said, "A word spoken in due season, how good is it!" (Prov. 15:23) Later, he wrote: "A word fitly spoken is like apples of gold in pictures of silver" (Prov. 25:11).

By allowing the Holy Spirit to tame your tongue and use it for God's glory, you can speak words of gold. Instead of wounding with your words, you will find yourself speaking tenderly, encouraging those who are down and comforting those who are distressed. You will be surprised at how the Lord uses simple truths that come from your lips to change the lives of others and build them up in the faith.

## AN IMPROVED MARRIAGE

"You changed our marriage with something you said in one of your sermons," a member of my church told me. This was a couple who had been married for a number of years, and I was surprised to get this good report.

Actually, what I had said had not been profound. I had simply pointed out that some in the congregation might be asking if they were getting all out of their marriages that they ought to be getting, but that was not the right question. "The right question," I said, "has to do with whether or not *your mate* is getting all out of the marriage that he or she ought to be getting."

I cannot tell you how much it meant to me to have had a part in building up that Christian marriage. That is the way our Lord works: As we enrich others, we are enriched too.

## YOUR HEART IS THE KEY

The first step in taming your tongue is the complete surrender of your heart to the Lord. When your heart is right, you will say the right things. Jesus said, "Out of the abundance of the heart the mouth speaketh. A good man out of the good treasure of the heart bringeth forth good things, and an evil man out of the evil treasure bringeth forth evil things" (Matt. 12:34-35).

Be sure that you have put away all bitterness. If you harbor bitter thoughts about others, bitter words are sure to come out when you least expect them. Forgive all who have wronged you. Root out all thoughts of revenge. Confess all wrong attitudes. Get thoroughly right with God and others. Abandon anger; cultivate love.

Especially avoid having negative feelings about any servant of God. Many Christians fall into this satanic trap. They begin to focus on the faults of their pastor or members of his family and soon join in little groups to grumble about the very ones they had ought to be upholding in prayer.

A.B. Simpson, founder of the Christian amd Missionary Alliance, said that he would rather take forked lightning or live electrical wires in his hands than to speak a reckless word against any servant of Christ. Such care in speaking about God's servants is rare, but you can be one who guards both heart and tongue against the sin of making verbal attacks upon servants of the Lord.

## HYPOCRISY HURTS

Avoid hypocrisy. Surrender totally to Christ. Be honest with God and man. Your transparency of life will keep you from an up and down Christian experience that would be likely to show up in what you say. James wrote: "Out of the same mouth proceedeth blessing and cursing. My brethren, these things ought not so to be. Doth a fountain send forth at the same place sweet water and bitter? Can the fig tree, my brethren, bear olive berries? Either a vine figs? So can no fountain both yield salt water and fresh" (James 3:10-12).

Commenting on this text, George Sweeting said:

> Nature has no confusion in her plans. A fountain sends forth sweet water or bitter. A fig tree bears figs; the vine bears grapes. But man, the highest of God's creatures, is confused. He blesses one day and curses the next.
>
> Words of praise and prayer come from the same tongue that spits poison. Are your words like the bitter waters of Marah?
>
> Then beseech the God of Moses to touch your tongue with the tree of Calvary and make the bitter sweet.[2]

## SILENCE IS GOLDEN

Learning the value of silence will also help you get your tongue under control. There are times to speak and times when it is better to be quiet and listen. Abraham Lincoln observed that is is better to remain silent and be thought a fool than to speak out and remove all doubt. But Solomon wrote of the positive side of silence: "Even a fool, when he holdeth his peace is counted wise, and he that shutteth his lips is esteemed a man of understanding" (Prov. 17:28).

Dr. William Osler called the ability to keep silent one of the finest of arts. He saw the atmosphere of life as being darkened by people murmuring over nonessentials and trifles that are inevitably part of life's routine and spoke of the value of cultivating quietude so as not to annoy others with our complaints.

As a pastor, I quickly saw the value of remaining silent when someone began talking about the faults of others.

Knowing that even one word of agreement might cause me to be quoted wrongly about the charges being made, I determined to keep quiet or tactfully maneuver the conversation to another subject.

Such tongue control does not come easily, especially if the complaints about the person in question are likely to be true. Ministers are as prone to judgment as others and find it human to join in a tirade against members who are argumentative or continually opposing the forward motion of the church. I found great help in keeping silent in the prayer of David for God to place a sentinel at his mouth to guard his lips lest he say things that he would later regret: "Set a watch, O Lord, before my mouth, keep the door of my lips" (Ps. 141:3).

The thought that God could dispatch a guard to keep me from speaking wrongly was just what I needed to enable me to remain silent when it would have been easier to express some negative opinion. I am confident that these times of silence have kept me from speaking unwisely on a number of matters and have delivered my congregations from strife over some criticism I might have made of one of the members in a moment of weakness or discouragement.

Words that gender strife are better left unsaid. Here especially, "silence is golden." James says words that produce bitterness and strife have an unholy source. His revelation of the satanic influence of bitterness, envy, and strife ought to be considered before one word contributing to these attitudes is spoken: "But if ye have bitter envying and strife in your hearts, glory not, and lie not against the truth. This wisdom descendeth not from above, but is earthly, sensual, devilish. For where envying and strife is, there is confusion and every evil work" (James 3:14-16).

## HELPFUL WORDS NEED TO BE SAID

On the other hand, words that bless and bring peace are from the Lord. Of these, James taught: "But the wisdom that is from above is first pure, then peaceable, gentle, and easy to be intreated, full of mercy and good fruits, without partiality, and without hypocrisy. And the fruit of righteousness is sown in peace of them that make peace" (James 3:17-18).

## THE POWER OF THE GOSPEL

Another important step in taming your tongue is to be busy sharing the Gospel with others. Evangelism is missing from too many churches on Sunday because so few Christians share the Gospel with others during the week.

"Why is it that we so seldom have anyone respond to the invitation to receive Christ as Saviour in our church?" a man asked.

"Probably because you so seldom have lost people in the Sunday services," I replied. And my answer would have been appropriate to members of most churches today.

We have developed many helpful seminars and teaching tools for successful living, but have somehow managed to minor on the most important task given to us by the risen Christ: that of telling the Gospel to those who are lost. Some estimate that 90 percent of all Christians have never led another person to Christ. How can we reconcile this poor performance with our Lord's commission to preach the Gospel to every creature?

How long has it been since you shared your faith with another person?

Most of the strife that paralyzes churches would end if the members began looking outward. Tongues that are busy sharing the Gospel are seldom used to share gossip. It is because we have so few going with the Gospel that church problems keep growing.

Recently, while speaking in a church Bible conference, I was asked to meet with a man who had been converted only a few months before the conference began. He had been faithful in every service and had brought others with him to the meetings.

During our session, he asked what he could do to keep from becoming like the other members of the church. Surprised, I asked what he meant.

He explained that those who had been in the church for a long time seemed to have little interest in reaching out to lost people. He was afraid that the influence of these "mature"

Christians might cause him to lose his compassion for the lost.

This new convert had raised a serious issue. Here was a church filled with good people who were very involved in the church program but who were not obeying the Great Commission (Matt. 28:18-20). They were caught up in keeping the church solvent and attending services but cared little for lost people in the community. The zealous new convert saw through the flurry of activity and feared he might get caught in the same trap.

## JUST GOING THROUGH THE MOTIONS

A woman once phoned and asked me to come to her home to lead her husband to Christ. He was ready to respond to the Gospel and had told her to call a minister.

Then she shocked me.

"I called another church," she said, giving the name of a fine church with three ordained men on the staff. "But no one could come because they're having an evangelistic service tonight."

My shock was not just over the failure of that church but over the thought of how easy it would be for any church to allow a program to take priority over individual needs. The people who attended that evangelistic service found it easier to be part of a group that gathered in a church meeting than to search out lost people and win them to Christ. Allegiance to a program, admirable as that may be, should never take the place of personally reaching out to those who need the Lord to share the Gospel with them.

## WATCH THOSE NEW CONVERTS

Some are honestly afraid to evangelize because they do not feel qualified, thinking they need a considerable amount of Bible training before seeking to win others to Christ. But this argument does not hold up because new converts generally reproduce themselves in the faith more quickly than those who have been Christians for many years. The main reason for this is their genuine concern for their friends who are lost and their willingness to speak to them about Christ. Their methods may not be the textbook type but they care and that important ingredient sends them out to reach others.

A man who had become a Christian started witnessing to his friends and was successful in leading many of them to Christ. One of the members of my church didn't approve of the new convert's methods of evangelism.

"He doesn't go about it right," the concerned member said.

"Don't tell him," I replied.

The man's methods may not have measured up but his results were great and I didn't want anyone holding him back.

People who are busy sharing their faith in Christ with others are so involved in doing the greatest work on earth that they have little time to be upset and edgy over trifles. Neither are they likely to speak offensively. After becoming involved in reaching others for Christ, they develop into tender people who are more interested in meeting needs than in having their own way.

Sharing the Gospel may be the key to taming your tongue. In doing so, you will begin to look beyond yourself and your disappointments. As you cultivate love for people in order to lead them to Christ, this same love will influence your tongue, causing you to speak with care so as not to lose opportunities to tell others about your Lord.

## KEEP PRAISING!

The psalmist gave another remedy for a tongue out of control: praising God continually. He declared: "I will bless the Lord at all times; His praise shall continually be in my mouth" (Ps. 34:1).

When we are occupied with praising God, we will have no interest in putting down others. C.H. Spurgeon said we ought to praise God more and blame neighbors less. But one of these practices naturally follows the other: as we give ourselves to thoughts and words of praise, we will be less likely to blame others for our difficulties.

David's resolution to praise God continually is the verbalizing of Paul's call to occupy our minds with thoughts of praise: "Finally, brethren, whatsoever things are true, whatsoever things are honest, whatsoever things are just, whatsoever things are pure, whatsoever things are lovely, whatsoever things are of good report; if there be any virtue, and if there be any praise, think on these things" (Phil. 4:8).

Oscar Van Impe, father of Evangelist Jack Van Impe, is known as a man who is always praising the Lord. This has been true since his conversion and was the cause of some ridicule in the automobile plant where he worked at that time.

"Praise the Lord!" some fellow workers would shout when Oscar entered their area of the plant.

"Amen, but I wish you meant it like I do!" was his usual reply.

During Jack's teen years, he once had a minor accident with his father's car and decided to put Oscar's Christian joy to the test. Coming into the house after the incident, he shouted, "Praise the Lord, Dad! I had an accident with the car."

Oscar's response was characteristic of the new man he had become. Placing his arm around Jack's shoulder, he replied, "Praise the Lord, Son! We're not going to let the devil have the victory!"

Jack was so impressed with his father's positive reaction that he has shared it with thousands when giving his conversion story in large crusades. Oscar's response was entirely different than it would have been before his conversion, for upon receiving Christ as his Saviour, he became so thrilled with his Lord that continual praise seemed only natural, and he has busied his tongue with words of praise ever since.[3]

## A.W. TOZER'S CURE FOR A WAYWARD TONGUE

Praise is the voicing of thanksgiving, going beyond just appreciation of things to adoration of the Lord, the giver. And a thankful heart will keep an otherwise wayward tongue under control. A.W. Tozer wrote: "Now as a cure for the sour, faultfinding attitude, I recommend the cultivation of the habit of thankfulness. Thanksgiving has great curative power. The heart that is constantly overflowing with gratitude will be safe from those attacks of resentfulness and gloom that bother so many religious persons. A thankful heart cannot be cynical.

"We should never take any blessing for granted, but accept everything as a gift from the Father of Lights. Whole days may be spent occasionally in the holy practice of being thankful. We should write on a tablet one by one the things for which we are grateful to God and to our fellowmen. And a constant return to this thought during the day as our minds get free will serve to fix the habit in our hearts."[4]

While, as James says, some bless God and curse men, it is impossible to do both at the same time. The time we use praising the Lord will not be available for wounding others with our words. And as we increase our times of praise, the habit of praise will have a positive effect on what we say.

## A PRAYER FOR VICTORY

We do not have to be victims of our own voices, forever filled with regret over harsh or hasty words. Human nature cannot tame the tongue of man, but as believers who are indwelt by the Holy Spirit and instructed by the Bible we can achieve such control that David's prayer for proper thinking and speaking will often be in our hearts and on our lips: "Let the words of my mouth and the meditation of my heart be acceptable in Thy sight, 0 Lord, my strength, and my Redeemer" (Ps. 19:14).

# TEN

# CONFRONTING YOUR REAL ENEMY

During the high school graduation season, I saw a car painted for the occasion. The year of graduation stood out in bold numbers across the trunk lid, accompanied by a list of class desires. It was the printing on the driver's door that startled me: "WE PARTY WITH THE DEVIL."

Too many people party with the devil.

But partying is not the devil's only activity. Night and day, he is busy in every area of our lives. And he may be most dangerous when operating in areas where he is not easily identified.

## OUR ADVERSARY

The Apostle Peter called the devil our adversary and compared him to a roaring lion, roaming about seeking victims: "Be sober, be vigilant, because your adversary the devil, as a roaring lion walketh about, seeking whom he may devour" (1 Peter 5:8).

Peter gave his warning about our adversary immediately after urging his readers to get rid of their cares. Evidently, we are most vulnerable to the devil's attacks when we are burdened down with anxiety. In order to make daily victory over Satan possible, Peter called for giving all care to the One who cares for us: "Casting all your care upon Him, for He careth for you" (1 Peter 5:7).

## THE DECEIVER

Among other things, Paul spoke of the devil as a deceiver (2 Cor. 11:3). Perhaps our enemy's greatest deception is revealed in the image he has given the world of himself. Many see him as the instigator of good times—an imaginary character to joke about. But nothing could be further from the truth. He is a real being whose aim is our destruction.

## LIAR, MURDERER, THIEF

Jesus called the devil a murderer and a liar. Speaking to the Pharisees, He said: "Ye are of your father the devil, and the lusts of your father ye will do. He was a murderer from the beginning, and abode not in the truth, because there is no truth in him. When he speaketh a lie, he speaketh of his own, for he is a liar, and the father of it" (John 8:44).

Contrasting His own purpose in the world to that of the devil, He declared: "The thief cometh not, but for to steal, and to kill, and to destroy; I am come that they might have life, and that they might have it more abundantly" (John 10:10).

## VISITING SKID ROW

While a student at Moody Bible Institute, I had my first view of Chicago's Skid Row. Since I grew up in rural Michigan, this was a real eye-opener to me. Here I saw people who appeared to be at the end of the road, and one of the most interesting facts to me about them was the variety of their backgrounds.

I learned that many of these hurting ones were well educated. A number of them were professionals who at one time had high hopes of success. Now they were on the bottom rung of life's ladder, holding on day after day but having few reasons for doing so.

They had been robbed of nearly all of the important things in life. Most had lost their families and friends as well as their health. Many were like moving corpses, shuffling about from place to place but without real life. They were prime examples of those who had been victimized by Satan, the thief and murderer.

On that first visit to Skid Row, I tried earnestly to tell a man about Christ and what He could do for him. The fellow claimed to have been a dentist before his downward slide.

When it became clear that I wasn't getting through, I told him that I would pray for him.

"Don't do that," he begged; "the last time anyone prayed for me I had all kinds of trouble."

Here was a mind-boggling situation. This broken man had lost most of the things that count in life. He was being given an opportunity to make a new start, to have his record cleared with God, and his future assured. The prayers of others had convinced him that God exists and that circumstances can be affected by calling on Him. Still, he would not respond to God's love by receiving Christ as his personal Saviour.

More than thirty years have passed since my encounter with the Skid Row dentist. During that time, I've observed Satan the thief at work in the lives of many people at different levels of society. I'm now convinced that the purposes of this enemy never change and that he still seeks to steal all that is good from our lives, filling them instead with sorrow, heartache, and despair.

## SATANIC ACTIVITY TODAY

Today, families are under satanic attack. Perhaps your family has been affected by the Deceiver's strategy. The thief may have stolen love and tranquility from your once happy home.

While there certainly is reason for concern, we should remember that Satan's attack on families is not new. Our first parents were deceived like many today, losing the joy and fellowship of Eden. Shortly after that, the first sons of Adam and Eve were at war (Gen. 4:1-15). And the casualties of that battle continue.

Paul explained that Satan feeds lust and fans the flames of immorality. He wrote: "And you hath He quickened, who were dead in trespasses and sins; wherein in time past ye walked according to the course of this world, according to the prince of the power of the air, the spirit that now worketh in the children of disobedience, among whom also we all had our conversation in times past in the lusts of our flesh, fulfilling the desires of the flesh and of the mind, and were by nature the children of wrath, even as others" (Eph. 2:1-3).

Now get this shocker: *Anything that promotes lust is of the devil.*

Satan deals in lust. It is his stock-in-trade. This includes lust that looks toward immorality, lust for riches or position or power. James says: "Then when lust hath conceived, it bringeth forth sin; and sin, when it is finished, bringeth forth death" (James 1:15).

You may have relegated Satan to the wild parties envisioned by reading the sign on the high-school senior's car door, to the dark rooms and alleys of Skid Row, or to cultic followers of Satan. He is certainly involved in these, but he is also active in the more respectable and accepted areas of life when lust is the merchandiser or the tool used to capture and hold attention.

## THE DESTROYER

Satan is a destroyer. It is his purpose to destroy your health, your life, your home, your country. His purpose will never change.

Note Paul's description of Satanic activity in the last days:

> This know also, that in the last days perilous times shall come. For men shall be lovers of their own selves, covetous, boasters, proud, blasphemers, disobedient to parents, unthankful, unholy, without natural affection, trucebreakers, false accusers, incontinent, fierce, despisers of those that are good, traitors, heady, highminded, lovers of pleasures more than lovers of God; having a form of godliness, but denying the power thereof: from such turn away (2 Tim. 3:1-5).

Look back to Eden, and you will find Satan using lust for self-gratification to destroy people. Look ahead to the second coming of Christ and you will find Satan using lust for power to destroy people, with the intention of destroying Christ Himself: "And I saw the beast, and the kings of the earth, and their armies, gathered together to make war against Him that sat on the horse, and against His army" (Rev. 19:19).

Look about you and you will see evidences of the tempter at work on every hand. In your own life, be alert for his disguised advances.

C.H. Spurgeon wrote: "Satan shows the bait but hides the hook. He is far too crafty to let men see the naked sin, or the unveiled punishment. He covers the hook with the bait of pleasure, or profit, or philosophy, or progress, or even piety."[1]

The owner of a Christian bookstore surprised me with her comment about books revealing the tactics of Satan. She refused to stock them, feeling that if she ignored the devil, he would not bother her. This view doesn't square with the instruction given in the Bible for overcoming our enemy. We are to become aware of his methods so that we can avoid his traps (2 Cor. 2:11).

## A POWERFUL ENEMY

We must be on guard continually, remembering that we face a formidable foe, one who was able to deceive Eve in the perfect environment of the Garden of Eden and who has led many others astray through the centuries. This enemy may even use religion to accomplish his purposes. Paul warned: "For such are false apostles, deceitful workers, transforming themselves into the apostles of Christ. And no marvel, for Satan himself is transformed into an angel of light. Therefore it is no great thing if his ministers also be transformed as the ministers of righteousness, whose end shall be according to their works" (2 Cor. 11:13-15).

Let us understand then that Satan works in all the areas of conflict we have discussed. He is the prime mover in temptation. He works to keep believers from forgiving one another, causing the loss of personal blessings and local church power. He attempts to keep the children of God in an anxious state of mind so that they cannot serve their Lord effectively. He delights in untamed tongues that keep gossip flowing and Christians divided.

From a human standpoint, Satan's power is immense. Some teach that the devil cannot perform miracles, but this view overlooks the facts. Satan spoke through the mouth of the serpent in the temptation of Eve and this was just the first of many Satanic miracles recorded in the Bible.

When Moses and Aaron appeared before Pharaoh and worked miracles in the power of God, a number of these were duplicated by the Egyptian magicians. The miracles performed by the magicians were undoubtedly the work of Satan (Ex. 7-8).

Nor will this evil power diminish in the future. In the Book of Revelation, John says the coming false prophet of the end time will have miracle-working power from Satan that will enable him to deceive many:

> And he doeth great wonders, so that he maketh fire come down from heaven on the earth in the sight of men, and deceiveth them that dwell on the earth by the means of those miracles which he had power to do in the sight of the beast; saying to them that dwell on the earth, that they should make an image to the beast, which had the wound by a sword, and did live. And he had power to give life unto the image of the beast, that the image of the beast should both speak, and cause that as many as would not worship the image of the beast should be killed (Rev. 13:13-15).

Satan's titles still sound impressive. He is called "the god of this world" (2 Cor. 4:4) and the "prince of the power of the air" (Eph. 2:2). During the temptation of Jesus, Satan touted his earthly power by offering our Lord the kingdoms of this world if He would fall down and worship him (Matt. 4:8-9). Perhaps the Epistle of Jude contains the most awesome demonstration of the power of Satan, one that tempers my language when dealing with this enemy: "Yet Michael the archangel, when contending with the devil he disputed about the body of Moses, durst not bring against him a railing accusation, but said, 'The Lord rebuke thee'" (Jude 9).

Thankfully, we are equipped to win over this powerful evil one who desires our destruction. The indwelling Holy Spirit is more powerful than our enemy. John wrote: "Ye are of

God, little children, and have overcome them, because greater is He that is in you, than he that is in the world" (1 John 4:4).

## FORMULA FOR VICTORY

While we could never stand against so powerful a foe as Satan in our own strength, our Lord provides power for victory when we surrender completely to Him. James gave the following formula for victory over the devil: "Submit yourselves therefore to God. Resist the devil, and he will flee from you" (James 4:7).

Notice the order of action in this formula: first submission to God, then resistance of the devil. It is vital that we follow this pattern. Attempts to resist the devil without submitting to God are sure to fail.

F.B. Meyer wrote:

> There is only one way by which the tempter can be met. He laughs at our good resolutions and ridicules the pledges with which we fortify ourselves. There is only One whom he fears; One who in the hour of greatest weakness conquered him; and who has been raised far above all principality and power, that He may succor and deliver all frail and tempted souls.[2]

Do you feel frail and tempted? Then follow the formula for victory: Submit to God and resist the devil. Upon doing so, you will win over your enemy. God guarantees that Satan will flee from you. Victory will be yours—every time.

## THE POWER OF CHRIST'S DEATH

The victory of Christ on the cross should be another source of comfort to us when we are under attack. In his book *Satan, Satanism and Witchcraft*, Richard DeHaan says:

> The Lord Jesus sealed Satan's defeat and eternal condemnation when He paid the full price for human sin on the cross and, as the God-man, destroyed the power of death by His resurrection. Therefore, though the devil is

still called "the god of this world" and at this very time "goes about like a roaring lion seeking whom he may devour," he knows he cannot win his war against God. In fact, he cannot even cause a humble believer to sin if that individual submits to God and opposes the evil one. The devil is far more powerful than any person, and the individual who tries to defeat him in his own strength will surely fail. The Christian who lives in daily submission to the Lord, however, can successfully resist every onslaught of Satan.[3]

We will do well to appropriate the power of the blood of Christ to overcome Satan. I start every day claiming that power.

Note this important message about overcoming Satan that John heard and recorded for us:

And the great dragon was cast out, that old serpent, called the devil, and Satan, which deceiveth the whole world: he was cast out into the earth, and his angels were cast out with him. And I heard a loud voice saying in heaven, "Now is come salvation, and strength, and the kingdom of our God, and the power of His Christ, for the accuser of our brethren is cast down, which accused them before our God day and night. And they overcame him by the blood of the Lamb, and by the word of their testimony; and they loved not their lives unto the death" (Rev. 12:9-11).

Evangelist Dwight L. Moody told about a visit to a man in Dundee, Scotland who had broken his back in a fall and had been confined to his bed for forty years. Moody was amazed at the man's inward joy and described him as one of the happiest men he had ever met, saying he wondered if angels passing over Dundee might have stopped at the man's bed to be refreshed.

Upon being asked if he was ever tempted by Satan to think that God was a hard Master and didn't really love him, the bedfast believer admitted that those times did occasionally come to him. He explained that these potential periods of defeat usually came when he saw others prospering and in good health. But he added that he had learned he could handle these attacks by taking the tempter to the cross and showing him Christ and His wounds as proof of God's love. "Satan got such a scare there hundreds of years ago," he said, "that he cannot stand it; he leaves me every time."[4]

We have a real and powerful enemy. He knows our weak spots and is quick to attack us in them. But we are not destined for defeat. The Holy Spirit lives within us and is greater in power than our enemy. Our Saviour defeated Satan at the cross. His death and resurrection provide complete victory when we appropriate His power by faith. Through total submission to God and determined resistance to Satan, we can overcome the one who seeks our defeat.

## FAITH IS THE VICTORY

Sharing concepts to overcome Satan in his book *Satan's Angels,* Ken Anderson wrote:

> The closer a Christian walks with his Lord, the more conscious he will become of satanic interference. In my own experiences, I have come to often say to myself, "Well, there he is again." Invariably when God gives me a special opportunity to serve Him, Satan appears on the scene. But no matter! Through the simple exercise of faith, I have authority over Satan![5]

That same authority is available to every Christian. Awesome as the power of Satan may be, we need not fear. Our Lord will shelter us in His love, arm us for every conflict, and enable us to win.

# ELEVEN
# PREPARED TO FIGHT

When you became a Christian, you thought your troubles were over. Then reality moved in. Though you had become a child of God, possessing eternal life and having the assurance of a home in heaven, you still had certain aggravations and struggles here below.

Temptation remained a problem. You may have even found yourself having more temptations than before you came to Christ.

The reason? As a believer, you became a prime target for the tempter. Your newfound faith enlisted you in a lifelong battle against the forces of evil. Paul explained: "For we wrestle not against flesh and blood, but against principalities, against powers, against the rulers of the darkness of this world, against spiritual wickedness in high places" (Eph. 6:12).

Sounds scary! Not only must we contend with the devil, but with a whole host of demonic powers that serve under him. Yet there is a bright side to this disturbing revelation: Christ equips us for the battle. We are prepared to fight.

## ENCOURAGING WORDS
In his provocative book *The Whole Armor of God,* Albert Hughes wrote:

It must be clear to us all by this time that the Christian life is one of constant conflict. It is a strenuous struggle from start to finish. Those who expect to be carried to heaven on flowery beds of ease are living in a fool's paradise. The Scripture states clearly that we must contend every foot of the way. One thing, however, that the Ephesian epistle makes clear is that we are to be conquerors. We are always to face the encounter *in Christ,* and thus we can win.[1]

## A LONG BATTLE

J.C. Ryle called the believer's conflict a fight of perpetual necessity and described it as follows:

It admits of no breathing time, no armistice, no truce. On weekdays as well as on Sundays—in private as well as in public—at home by the family fireside as well as abroad—in little things like management of tongue and temper, as well as in great ones like the government of kingdoms—the Christian's warfare must unceasingly go on. The foe we have to do with keeps no holidays, never slumbers, and never sleeps. So long as we have breath in our bodies, we must keep on our armor, and remember we are on an enemy's ground. "Even on the brink of Jordan," said a dying saint, "I find Satan nibbling at my heels." We must fight till we die.[2]

So the fight is on. And it is vital that we win every day. Our own peace of mind and joy in living depends on moving from victory to victory. Spiritual defeats are costly. They can bring depression, affect our families, reduce our usefulness in the Lord's service, and cancel the effectiveness of our witness to others.

## WINNING OR LOSING AFFECTS OTHERS

My visit to the home of a man who had but a short time to live was at the request of his daughter. Her concern for him was intensified by his repeated claims of unbelief. Communication with this man was difficult because his illness had affected his ability to speak. Though he was able to handle some conversation, most of his responses to my questions and comments were made on a lap-sized blackboard.

While this slowed our exchange of thoughts, it gave ample time to consider each statement. And in this case, I was eager to make every word count.

The imminency of death had not shaken unbelief from this troubled man. Having built his case over a period of years, he was not about to be stampeded into faith in Christ.

Most of his convictions were based on what he thought to be the injustices of God, especially concerning the suffering of righteous people. A relative, who had been a zealous Christian, had suffered long with a serious illness, a fact he could not reconcile with the existence of a loving God. As a result, he insisted on retaining faith in his doubts.

Then I dropped the bomb that shattered his unbelief. Knowing that his daughter had been genuinely converted and feeling confident that her life demonstrated her faith, I asked: "Is there anything about the change in your daughter's life that you cannot explain apart from the work of God?"

Suddenly the old arguments about God's injustice were inadequate. The skeptic had seen evidence of new life in his daughter, and all the logic of his unbelief could not stand up before that living example. An ounce of testimony had proved to be worth more than a pound of argument. The daughter's daily victory conquered her father's unbelief.

## STRENGTH FROM ABOVE

Since it is so vital that we win in this spiritual conflict, it will be important to understand that our Lord has provided exactly what we need for the battle. But before considering our spiritual equipment, let us be reminded that our strength for the conflict will come from the Lord. Paul said: "Finally, my brethren, be strong in the Lord, and in the power of His might" (Eph. 6:10).

Our enemies are strong but our Lord is all powerful. They are of high rank, being called principalities, powers, and rulers of the darkness of this world. But Jesus occupies the highest place of all.

Consider this faith-building text:

> And what is the exceeding greatness of His power to usward who believe, according to the working of His mighty power, which He wrought in Christ, when He raised Him from the dead, and set Him at His own right hand in the heavenly places, far above all principality, and power, and might, and dominion, and every name that is named, not only in this world, but also in that which is to come; and hath put all things under His feet, and gave Him to be the head over all things to the church, which is His body, the fullness of Him that filleth all in all (Eph. 1:19-23).

"Be strong" would be an impossible command to obey if the power of Christ was not available to us. Our enemy is too powerful for us to withstand. But the power and position of Christ changes all that. We are able to stand against any foe because His power is in us and operates through us.

A minister who had been troubled by periods of depression and weakness told me that he had overcome these distressing times by remembering that Jesus is higher than all satanic powers.

"Satan is the prince of the power of the air," he said, "but Christ is far above all principalities and powers. When the devil attacks, I just ask the Lord to pick him off from above."

## THE ARMOR OF GOD

In addition to providing His strength to compensate for our weakness, our Lord has given us equipment with which to fight against the powers of darkness. Paul calls this the "armor of God" and urges all believers to make full use of it: "Put on the whole armor of God, that ye may be able to stand against the wiles of the devil" (Eph. 6:11). And, "Wherefore take unto you the whole armor of God, that ye may be able to withstand in the evil day, and having done all, to stand" (Eph. 6:13).

Paul then describes this fighting equipment piece by piece so that we can understand how practical it is and be able to use it every day. He writes:

> Stand therefore, having your loins girt about with truth, and having on the breastplate of righteousness; and having your feet shod with the preparation of the Gospel of peace; above all, taking the shield of faith, wherewith ye shall be able to quench all the fiery darts of the wicked. And take the helmet of salvation, and the sword of the Spirit, which is the Word of God, praying always with all prayer and supplication in the Spirit, and watching thereunto with all perseverence and supplication for all saints (Eph. 6:14-18).

## THE GIRDLE OF TRUTH

Jesus called the devil the father of lies (John 8:44). Paul says truthfulness is vital in opposing him and names the girdle of truth as the first piece of armor that is necessary for the believer's protection in battle.

Truth keeps us from harmful entanglements. No one has a good enough memory to be a successful liar. Sooner or later dishonesty will destroy us. If we are to stand against the father of lies and his forces, we must choose truth.

We need to be honest with ourselves, with God, and with others. The enemy delights to have us stay purposely blind to our own sins. The Pharisees had fallen into this trap. They continually focused on the sins of others while magnifying their own religious acts and this produced spiritual pride and blindness. Personal victory depends on facing our sins and confessing them (1 John 1:9).

While seeking revival in the Hebrides, a group of Christians prayed together in a barn, three nights a week, for months. Finally, after reading Psalm 24, one young man closed his Bible and said: "Brethren, it is just so much humbug to be waiting thus night after night, month after month, if we ourselves are not right with God. I must ask myself—'Is my heart pure? Are my hands clean?' "[3] Conviction of personal dishonesty about facing up to sin had broken through bringing truth and only then did the long awaited revival come.

In his moving prayer of confession, David said, "Behold

thou desirest truth in the inward parts, and in the hidden part Thou shalt make me to know wisdom" (Ps. 51:6). Having lost a critical battle with the tempter, David realized the value of being totally honest with God. Such honesty practiced earlier might have kept him from falling into sin.

Being truthful does not mean that we should always tell all we know. Some things are better left unsaid. Once while visiting a man in the hospital, I found him upset over what had been said by a pastor who had visited him earlier. The pastor had told him that he was occupying the bed in which his neighbor had died the previous week. Honesty did not require that this depressing information be revealed.

Since the figure in this text is a military one, we should note that the girdle worn by a soldier was also for protection. Describing the military girdle, Albert Hughes wrote:

> We must not think of this as being only a belt like our soldiers wear on the outside of a military tunic. The girdle was more a piece of armor than an ornament. It was strongly made, of leather with metal plates all over it. When put on the person, it covered the whole of the lower part of the body. The girdle greatly helped the soldier to stand firmly on the ground, and it also saved the lower part of the body from injury.[4]

Dishonesty places us in jeopardy. Truth protects us when we are attacked. Since Christ is "the truth" (John 14:6), He can enable us to be truthful. Transparent honesty is vital if we are to win the battle against our wicked foes.

## THE BREASTPLATE OF RIGHTEOUSNESS

The second part of the believer's armor is called "the breast-plate of righteousness." Paul may have looked up from his writing to see a Roman soldier walking past, having on a breastplate, a coat of mail that covered him from his neck down to his hips.

Just what is the breastplate of righteousness? Some think it refers to the imputed righteousness that all believers receive upon being born again. Others think this has to do with our own righteousness after conversion. Probably both are in view.

We are most vulnerable to Satan's attacks when we are discouraged or depressed. Often these down times come as a result of our failure to do right. We know better but do wrong things. Words not fitting for the children of God flow from our lips. Thoughts not proper for Christians to entertain linger in our minds. Envy rears its ugly head. Good intentions are not carried through. As a result, our self-worth nose-dives.

Recently, I saw a familiar bumper sticker that says: "Christians are not perfect . . . just forgiven." I needed that encouraging message right then and gave thanks for it.

When these times of failure come, we can rise above them by resting in the righteousness of Christ. His righteousness became ours the moment we received Him as Saviour. Paul wrote: "For He hath made Him to be sin for us, who knew no sin, that we might be made the righteousness of God in Him" (2 Cor. 5:21).

As a result of your faith in Christ, you have been clothed in His righteousness. Let that truth lift you from despair the next time you feel down about failing. But there is also a down-to-earth dimension to the breastplate of righteousness: through the power of the Holy Spirit we can do right.

We are saved by grace, apart from works, but our salvation equips us to live righteously:

> For we are his workmanship, created in Christ Jesus unto good works, which God hath before ordained that we should walk in them (Eph. 2:10).
> For the grace of God that bringeth salvation hath appeared to all men, teaching us that, denying ungodliness and worldly lusts, we should live soberly, righteously, and godly in this present world (Titus 2:11-12).

This is not to say that believers do not sometimes stumble along the way. Perfection awaits the coming of the Lord. But it is important to know that we are not born to lose. Victory is possible.

Recently, a man who is nearly eighty years of age told me his secret of happiness. "Life can be so good," he said, "if you just do right." He had learned the value of choosing to do right, and it had made his life full and happy. This kind of living also thwarts the purposes of the powers of darkness.

## THE CHRISTIAN SOLDIER'S FEET

Christians are not only prepared to withstand their powerful enemies by defending themselves but also to overcome them by advancing with the Gospel. Paul called this positive approach to the conflict, "having your feet shod with the preparation of the Gospel of peace" (Eph. 6:15). This simply means being prepared to share the Gospel with others and being actively involved in doing so. It is an expression related to "How beautiful are the feet of them that preach the Gospel of peace, and bring glad tidings of good things!" (Rom. 10:15)

In his book *The Soul Winner's Fire*, John R. Rice wrote:

> In war and in football we are told that the "best defense is a good offense." The Christian who retires from the field of battle, and lets souls go unhindered to hell, is not safe from temptation; rather he is in greater danger. The Christian who really puts up a fight against Satan, and snatches men as brands from the burning, will find that all about him God has put a wall of protection.
>
> How many times I have been almost defeated, discouraged, downhearted, without a message to preach; but when I gave myself to personal soul-winning and had the joy of seeing some saved, what a joy, what close touch with God! How much easier it is to pray when you win souls! How much easier it is to resist temptation when your feet are shod with the preparation of the Gospel of peace![5]

A young minister in his first church shared his frustrations with me. He was finding it difficult to develop sermons that were effective, though he was applying all the study and sermon preparation techniques he had learned in seminary.

"When these times come," I advised, "leave your study and go to some home to tell someone about Christ."

I spoke from experience. Many times when there has seemed to be no clear leading of the Lord about preaching or when satanic opposition has been so strong that I could not break through, I have abandoned my commentaries and gone out to talk with someone about Jesus. Often the needed insights for preaching have come to me while driving to my destination or upon my return.

A man who received Christ as his Saviour experienced many wonderful changes in his life. Still, he felt defeated because he was unable to stop smoking. He wanted to become active in the church visitation program but feared that his use of cigarettes would keep him from being effective.

I not only urged him to get involved in visitation outreach but took him with me so that I could teach him how to share the Gospel with others. One night, after leading a woman and her son to Christ, we returned to my study and knelt to pray, thanking God for the victories He had given and asking for one more: freedom from the habit that so burdened this new convert.

Soon after that the answer came. He was set free from the bondage of tobacco use. An important factor in achieving this victory was his concern for lost people and his willingness to prepare himself for getting involved in winning them to Christ.

## THE SHIELD OF FAITH

Now Paul moves to the part of the believer's armor that he says is vital to the effectiveness of all the others: "Above all, taking the shield of faith, wherewith ye shall be able to quench all the fiery darts of the wicked" (Eph. 6:16).

In battle, the shield bears the brunt of the enemy's attack. It keeps the missiles of the opposing forces from reaching the protective covering of the body.

You may be sure that the forces of darkness will launch their fiery darts at you. But faith appropriates the power of God to stop and quench them. It actually enlists the resources of God Himself to stand off the attack of the enemy.

A number of Old Testament texts speak of God as our shield. Here are some of them:

> After these things the word of the Lord came to Abram in a vision, saying, Fear not, Abram, I am thy shield, and thy exceeding great reward (Gen. 15:1).
> But Thou, 0 Lord, art a shield for me; my glory, and the lifter up of mine head (Ps. 3:3).
> Our soul waiteth for the Lord: He is our help and our shield (Ps. 33:20).
> For the Lord God is a sun and a shield; the Lord will give grace and glory: no good thing will He withhold from them that walk uprightly (Ps. 84:11).

A comforting truth rises from these verses and others: God is our shield in battle. By faith, we call upon Him in the struggles and conflicts of life, and He responds by quenching the fiery darts of our enemies. No wonder victory can be sure.

## THE HELMET OF SALVATION

The final piece of battle clothing described by Paul is called "the helmet of salvation." Since the helmet protects the brain, it refers to the "know so" dimension of salvation.

Dwight L. Moody said he had never known anyone who was effective in serving Christ who did not have assurance of his salvation. Though the new birth takes place as the result of faith that springs from the heart (Rom. 10:10), it is so real that the Christian also has an intellectual certainty that it has taken place. He knows it. And the Bible confirms that he can know it. John wrote: "These things have I written unto you that believe on the name of the Son of God; that ye may know that ye have eternal life, and that ye may believe on the name of the Son of God" (1 John 5:13).

Assurance of salvation makes us bold. It imparts confidence; keeps us aware of who we are.

We are the people of God, children of the King. There is no need for us to cringe and cower before our enemies, powerful though they may be. Our Lord will protect us in battle and enable us to win. Let us therefore be calm under fire, expecting victory. Writing to the troubled believers in Corinth, Paul said: "But thanks be to God, which giveth us the victory through our Lord Jesus Christ. Therefore, my beloved brethren, be ye steadfast, unmoveable, always abounding in the work of the Lord, forasmuch as ye know that your labor is not in vain in the Lord" (1 Cor. 15:57-58).

## THE SWORD OF THE SPIRIT

Only one weapon is placed in the hand of the Christian soldier: "the sword of the Spirit, which is the Word of God" (Eph. 6:17). But this one weapon is sufficient. It was the one used by Jesus during His temptation in the desert (Matt. 4:1-11) and it will be all we need for every battle we face.

As a young Christian, I was thrilled to discover how effective the Bible could be in times of temptation. Verses that I had read or heard would come to my mind just when I needed them. I was learning to use the sword of the Spirit in the time of battle. This is a valuable lesson to learn and many fall prey to the tempter because they miss or neglect it.

Daily Bible study is absolutely essential to personal victory. Much as a soldier learns to handle his weapon, we need to become familiar with the sword of the Spirit. Memorizing Bible verses so that they are ready for use when we are under attack can make the difference between winning and losing.

How does one use the sword in battle? By quoting Bible verses that have to do with the current conflict. For example, when tempted by materialism, you might use the following:

> Lay not up for yourselves treasures upon earth, where moth and rust doth corrupt and where thieves break through and steal, but lay up for yourselves treasures in heaven, where neither moth nor rust doth corrupt, and where thieves do not break through nor steal: For where your treasure is, there will your heart be also (Matt. 6:19-21).

> Set your affection on things above and not on things of the earth (Col. 3:2).

> Seeing then that all these things shall be dissolved, what manner of persons ought ye to be in all holy conversation and godliness (2 Peter 3:11).

Whatever the temptation, there is a Bible text to deal with it. The sword of the Spirit is an adequate weapon for any battle against the enemy. Those who learn to use it well can expect to win.

## CONSTANT PRAYER

After explaining that the Christian soldier is equipped for both defense and victory, Paul stresses the importance of prayer: "Praying always with all supplication in the Spirit, and watching thereunto with all perseverance and supplication for all saints" (Eph. 6:18).

Prayer is the believer's line of communication with his heavenly Commander—and it is vital to victory. In his book *The Glory of His Grace*, William Hazer Wrighton wrote: "Prayer is the strategy of victory. We pray for our Lord's direction and command; for reinforcements, as Wellington prayed for Blucher to come to the field of Waterloo; for heaven's barrage; and for our comrades in battle, all the saints."[6]

When the going gets tough and you are about to despair, remember that God answers prayer. His ear is always open to your call. You can pray without ceasing and He will never tire of hearing from you.

## LUTHER'S LESSON

Martin Luther was once passing through a severe trial and felt depressed. The struggle against the enemy seemed too much for him. Sensing his despair, his wife dressed in black and entered his study, saying: "God is dead!"

"Nonsense, woman, God lives!" answered Luther.

"If you believe that God is living, act like it! Live like it!" she replied.[7]

Let us face every battle believing that our living Lord really cares and that He will bring us through to victory. That is His promise to all who trust in Him (2 Cor. 2:14).

# TWELVE
# HIGHER GROUND

Upon stepping out of the elevator, I made my way down the wide hospital corridor and saw the man I had come to visit standing outside the door of his room. He had been a patient there for three weeks as the result of an accident at work. A pressurized line on a machine had burst, sending hot liquid plastic into one of his eyes. It had been an extremely painful injury, and for a time his sight had been in jeopardy; but he had made good progress and was now being sent home to complete his recovery.

During his hospital stay, I had tried to lead this man to Christ but had been unsuccessful. Now I made another attempt but found him still unwilling to respond to the Gospel. Sensing that pressing him for a decision would be futile and unwise, I gently reminded him that the death of Christ on the cross proved God's love for him and that by simple faith he could receive the Lord as his Saviour. He thanked me for my concern and said that he hoped others would turn to Christ as a result of my ministry, though he was unwilling to do so.

Following his release from the hospital, the man visited his mother, who lived in a rural area in one of the Southern states. He was still unable to return to work and thought the time with her would be good for him.

His mother was a Christian, and a prayer meeting was to be held in her home during the time of his stay there. The small church she attended conducted its midweek prayer services in the homes of members and that was the week for her to open her house to the meeting.

As the neighbors began arriving for prayer, the Northern visitor found himself feeling uncomfortable about being there and asked to be excused from the meeting, intending to spend that time alone in another room. But the pleas of those who had come to pray were so earnest that he could not resist them. Reluctantly, he stayed with the group for prayer.

Surrounded by kneeling people, my friend remembered our hospital corridor conversation. He thought about God's love that had sent Jesus to the cross to die for him and concluded he should wait no longer to be right with the Lord.

## CROSSROADS

Describing his experience later, he said it was as if two roads stretched before him, one of them being God's way and the other the way to destruction. He decided to take the way of life and received Christ as his Saviour.

Even after conversion to Christ, there are crossroads ahead. All Christians go to heaven when they die but many miss the peace, joy, and personal victory that God wants them to have every day. Jesus wants us to have life "more abundantly" (John 10:10).

## ABUNDANT LIFE

Abundant life should be the goal of every believer. We should not settle for anything less than God's best. The yo-yo syndrome that keeps us "sometimes up and sometimes down" is *not* part of God's plan for His children. Still, even those who have become well known for their holiness of life and dynamic influence for Christ have often reached these heights after periods of spiritual struggle.

## J. HUDSON TAYLOR'S SEARCH

J. Hudson Taylor, founder of the China Inland Mission, wrestled with temptation and discouragement that almost drove him to despair. In a letter to his mother, he wrote:

I cannot tell you how I am buffeted sometimes by temptation. I never knew how bad a heart I have. Yet I do know that I love God and love His work, and desire to serve Him only and in all things. And I value above all else that precious Saviour in whom alone I can be accepted. Often I am tempted to think that one so full of sin cannot be a child of God at all. But I try to throw it back and rejoice all the more in the preciousness of Jesus and in the riches of the grace that has made us "accepted in the beloved." Beloved, He is of God; beloved, He ought to be of us. But, oh, how short I fall here again! May God help me love Him more and serve Him better. Do pray for me. Pray that the Lord will keep me from sin, will sanctify me wholly, will use me more largely in His service.[1]

Can this be the great J. Hudson Taylor? Tempted? Having a bad heart? Thinking himself too full of sin to be a child of God? Falling short in loving God?

Can you identify with his feelings?

## TAYLOR'S NEW LIFE

Six months after the above letter was written, a great change took place in Taylor's life. The change was so great that he declared God had made him a new man.

What brought about this change? It was a letter from another missionary who, like J. Hudson Taylor, had been seeking personal victory, greater faith, and increased holiness of life.

John McCarthy, the missionary, wrote to Taylor saying he had now concluded that striving, longing, and hoping for better days to come was not the way to holiness, happiness, or usefulness. Instead, he saw all of these things as being in Christ Himself and that trusting Him completely would provide all they had been seeking.

This simple but powerful truth transformed J. Hudson Taylor's life and ministry. As a result, he said he felt as if the dawning of a new and glorious day had risen upon him, adding that he seemed to have reached only the edge of a boundless sea. He now saw in Christ all he needed for power, for satisfaction of heart, and for unchanging joy. He wrote:

> How then to have our faith increased? Only by thinking of all that Jesus is and all He is for us: His life, His death, His work, He Himself as revealed to us in the Word, to be the subject of our constant thoughts. Not a striving to have faith . . . but a looking off to the Faithful One seems all we need; a resting in the Loved One entirely, for time and for eternity.[2]

In their book *Hudson Taylor's Spiritual Secret,* Dr. and Mrs. Howard Taylor wrote that where before J. Hudson Taylor had been a toiling burdened Christian with not much rest of soul, he now became a bright happy one, experiencing new power flowing through him and finding new peace. Troubles did not worry him as before. He had traded bondage for liberty and failure for victory. Fear and weakness had been replaced by a restful sense of sufficiency in Christ.

How interesting that such a choice servant of God struggled so long before discovering that the answer he sought was to be found in moment by moment trust in the Christ who had saved him! Yet millions of troubled believers miss this seemingly obvious truth just as Taylor did.

### NO SECRET

Dr. John Miles, president of Grand Rapids School of the Bible and Music, says one thing he dislikes about the book, *Hudson Taylor's Spiritual Secret,* is its title. He's concerned about readers concluding that victory in the Christian life is a secret instead of the exercise of childlike faith in Christ.

Dr. Miles makes a good point. And it seems to be the very point that Hudson Taylor was trying to make, as is shown in the following letter written to his sister after beginning to live the abundant life:

> The sweetest part, if one may speak of one part being sweeter than another, is the rest which full identification with Christ brings. I am no longer anxious about any-

thing, as I realize this; for He, I know, is able to carry out His will, and His will is mine. It makes no matter where He places me, or how. That is rather for Him to consider than for me; for in the easiest position He must give me grace, and in the most difficult His grace is sufficient.[3]

Sounds like total trust in all areas of life: nothing mysterious; nothing difficult to understand. The great missionary leader had simply learned to trust his Saviour for everything and this brought him both peace and power.

Childlike faith brings us to spiritual maturity. Recognizing this brings every temptation and trial within our power to conquer and every task within the range of our potential.

## HIS POWER FOR OUR WEAKNESS

Regardless of the task or test, we can do anything that is in the will of God for us to do. We do not have to settle for less than God's best. From a human standpoint, we may appear to be inadequate, but His power working through us compensates for our weakness (Phil. 4:13).

At one time, I found it difficult to speak or sing before groups without becoming extremely nervous. I seemed unable to conquer this unwanted fear.

Now I can minister to groups and church congregations large and small without becoming tense or fearful. While looking out across crowded auditoriums I am at ease.

Has my self-confidence increased over the years? Not at all. I rarely minister to people without thinking about how inadequate I am to meet their needs. What made the difference?

Long ago I exchanged my self-confidence for confidence in Christ. Self-confidence was doing little for me, so I discarded it, choosing instead to place my confidence in Christ for every situation. He has given me what I was unable to develop on my own. Since I know that He is in control, I can be relaxed, expecting Him to work His will through me.

## THE MIRACLES OF JESUS

Study the life and ministry of Jesus and see how ready He was to impart His blessings to those who asked.

A woman who had been sick for twelve years reached out and touched the hem of His garment and was made whole (Matt. 9:20-22). Two blind men voiced their faith in Him and received their sight (Matt. 9:27-31). A man with a withered hand stretched it forth and at a word from Jesus found it restored and just like his healthy one (Matt. 12:9-13). None of these miracles required conforming to some complicated spiritual prescription for healing. They all took place as the result of the Lord's response to childlike faith.

## THE TROUBLED PREACHER

A minister once came to see me because a cloud of depression seemed to hover continually over him. He wondered if life was worth living and had asked the Lord many times to end his earthly life and take him to heaven. In his search for answers, he had attended a number of "deeper life" conferences and when it was possible had met alone with the speakers in the hope of discovering the secret of personal victory.

Almost surprised at my own action, I handed this defeated preacher a Gospel of John and urged him to think of himself as a new Christian. I wanted him to return to the basics, refreshing his faith in the simplicity of the Gospel.

This proved to be exactly what he needed. Later, I heard him sharing his newfound victory with other ministers and telling them how it had come about. What the supposed "spiritual secrets" could not do was accomplished through a return to the simple message of Christ and His love.

## THE SIMPLICITY THAT IS IN CHRIST

Often I have been asked why there are so many long and difficult names in the Bible.

"Don't blame God," I always reply. "He started us off with an easy one: Adam."

And that is the way with the abundant life. God has made it easy and man has made it difficult. He has offered it through childlike faith, and man has complicated it with supposed secret and simplified prescriptions for happiness and power.

Do you long for daily victory? Stop striving and rest completely in Christ.

## CHRIST IS ALL

After ending his long search for victory, J. Hudson Taylor wrote: "Christ literally *all* seems to me now, the power, the only power for service, the only ground for unchanging joy."[4]

Paul wrote:

> As ye have therefore received Christ Jesus the Lord, so walk ye in Him, rooted and built up in Him, and stablished in the faith, as ye have been taught, abounding therein with thanksgiving. Beware lest any man spoil you through philosophy and vain deceit, after the tradition of men, after the rudiments of the world, and not after Christ. For in Him dwelleth all the fullness of the Godhead bodily. And ye are complete in Him, which is the head of all principality and power (Col. 2:6-10).

What could be clearer? Christ *really* is the answer. Your answer. He provides power for overcoming temptation, for putting away old hurts and grudges, for winning over worry, for taming your tongue. He makes daily victory over the powers of darkness possible. The armor of God for protection and conquest is received from His hand and strength for the battle is provided from His unlimited supply. In the times of fiercest conflict, He is with us. Not one of those who trust in Him will ever walk alone (Heb. 13:5-6).

## THE UPWARD WAY EVERY DAY

Lift your eyes to your heavenly Captain who leads you on to higher ground.

Stop feeling like a loser.

Expect victory.

As a Christian, you are equipped to win.

You can win!

## NOTES FOR CHAPTER ONE

1. Walter B. Knight, *Knight's Treasury of Illustrations,* Wm. B. Eerdmans Publishing Company, Grand Rapids, Michigan, 266.
2. Ibid., 262.
3. Gladys Hunt, *Ms. Means Myself,* Zondervan, Grand Rapids, Michigan, 59.
4. Walter B. Knight, *Knight's Master Book of New Illustrations,* Wm. B. Eerdmans Publishing Company, Grand Rapids, Michigan, 193.


## CHAPTER TWO

1. Walter B. Knight, *Knight's Master Book of New Illustrations,* William. B. Eerdmans Publishing Company, Grand Rapids, Michigan, 493.
2. A.W. Tozer, *Paths to Power,* Christian Publications, Harrisburg, Pennsylvania, 22-23.


## CHAPTER THREE

1. Charles A. Blanchard, *Getting Things from God,* The Bible Institute Colportage Association, Chicago, Illinois, 65.
2. Roger F. Campbell, *They Call Him the Walking Bible,* Action Press, div. of Thomas Nelson Publishers, Nashville, Tennessee, 151.
3. John R. Rice, *Prayer—Asking and Receiving,* Sword of the Lord Publishers, 151.
4. Watchman Nee, *Sit, Walk, Stand,* Christian Literature Crusade, Fort Washington, Pennsylvania, 62.


## CHAPTER FOUR

1. Dr. and Mrs. Howard Taylor, *Hudson Taylor's Spiritual Secret,* Moody Press, Chicago, Illinois, 33.
2. Ibid., 34-35.


## CHAPTER FIVE

1. Charlie Jones, *Life Is Tremendous,* Tyndale House Publishers, Inc., Wheaton, Illinois, 12.
2. Peg Rankin, *Yet I Will Trust Him,* Regal Books, Ventura, California, 1.
3. Ibid., 33.

## CHAPTER SIX

1. John R. Rice, *The King of the Jews*, Zondervan Publishing House, Grand Rapids, Michigan, 66-67.
2. Matthew Henry, *A Complete Bible Commentary*, Moody Press, Chicago, Illinois, 677.
3. Walter B. Knight, *Knight's Treasury of Illustrations*, Wm. B. Eerdmans Publishing Co., Grand Rapids, Michigan, 370.
4. Roger F. Campbell, *Let's Communicate*, Christian Literature Crusade, 189.
5. Jack Odell, *Here's How*, Pacific Garden Mission, Chicago, Illinois, 13.
6. M.R. DeHaan, *Studies in First Corinthians*, Zondervan Publishing House, Grand Rapids, Michigan, 118.


## CHAPTER SEVEN

1. H.C.G. Moule, *Ephesian Studies*, Pickering & Inglis Ltd., London, 236.
2. G.H. Lang, *The Parabolic Teaching of Scripture*, Wm. B. Eerdmans Publishing Company, Grand Rapids, Michigan, 160-161.
3. Richard Trench, *Notes on the Parables*, Baker Book House, Grand Rapids, Michigan, 55.
4. Wm. McCarrell, *Christ's Seven Last Words from the Cross*, Dunham Publishing Company, Findlay, Ohio, 3.
5. Walter B. Knight, *Knight's Treasury of Illustrations*, Wm. B. Eerdmans Publishing Company, Grand Rapids, Michigan, 360.
6. Roy Hession, *The Calvary Road*, Christian Literature Crusade, Fort Washington, Pennsylvania, 14-15.
7. Walter B. Knight, *Knight's Treasury of Illustrations*, Wm. B. Eerdmans Publishing Company, Grand Rapids, Michigan, 133.


## CHAPTER EIGHT

1. John Edmund Haggai, *How to Win over Worry*, Zondervan Publishing House, Grand Rapids, Michigan, 31.
2. Ibid., 31.
3. Bruce Larson, *There's a Lot More to Health than Not Being Sick*, Word Books, Waco, Texas, 14.
4. Walter B. Knight, *Knight's Treasury of Illustrations*, Eerdmans Publishing Company, Grand Rapids, Michigan, 189.
5. J.C. Ryle, *Holiness*, Fleming H. Revell, Old Tappan, New Jersey, 203.
6. Walter B. Knight, *Knight's Treasury of Illustrations*, Wm. B. Eerdmans Publishing Company, Grand Rapids, Michigan, 445.

## CHAPTER NINE

1. George Sweeting, *The Tongue—Angel or Demon?* Zondervan Publishing House, Grand Rapids, Michigan, 19.
2. Ibid., 24-25.
3. Roger F. Campbell, *They Call Him the Walking Bible,* Action Press (Thomas Nelson Publishers), Nashville, Tennessee, 64-65.
4. A.W. Tozer, *The Root of the Righteous,* Christian Publications, Inc., Harrisburg, Pennsylvania, 123-124.

## CHAPTER TEN

1. C.H. Spurgeon, *Spurgeon's Proverbs and Sayings with Notes,* Baker Book House, Grand Rapids, Michigan, 136.
2. Walter B. Knight, *Three Thousand Illustrations for Christian Service,* Wm. B. Eerdmans Publishing Company, Grand Rapids, Michigan, 234-235.
3. Richard W. DeHaan, *Satan, Satanism, and Witchcraft,* Zondervan Publishing House, Grand Rapids, Michigan, 18.
4. Walter B. Knight, *Three Thousand Illustrations for Christian Service,* Wm. B. Eerdmans Publishing Company, Grand Rapids, Michigan, 233.
5. Ken Anderson, *Satan's Angels,* Thomas Nelson Publishers, Nashville, Tennessee, 151.

## CHAPTER ELEVEN

1. Albert Hughes, *The Whole Armor of God,* Zondervan Publishing House, Grand Rapids, Michigan, 33.
2. J. C. Ryle, *Holiness,* Fleming H. Revell Company, Old Tappan, New Jersey, 56.
3. Stephen F. Oldford, *Heart Cry for Revival,* Fleming H. Revell, Old Tappan, New Jersey, 28-29.
4. Albert Hughes, *The Whole Armor of God,* Zondervan Publishing House, Grand Rapids, Michigan, 46.
5. John R. Rice, *The Soul Winner's Fire,* Moody Press, Chicago, Illinois, 113.
6. William Hazer Wrighton, *The Glory of His Grace,* Zondervan Publishing House, Grand Rapids, Michigan, 122.
7. Walter B. Knight, *Knight's Treasury of Illustrations,* Wm. B. Eerdmans Publishing Company, 422.

## CHAPTER TWELVE

1. Dr. and Mrs. Howard Taylor, *Hudson Taylor's Spiritual Secret,* Moody Press, Chicago, Illinois, 153

2. Ibid., 156.
3. Ibid., 162.
4. Ibid., 156.

To get the author's cassette *Faith Builders for Your Down Days,* Send $5.00 to:

Rev. Roger Campbell
P.O. Box 444
Waterford, MI 48095